S*I*ZE

DOES MATTER

GROW YOUR BUSINESS, THINKING BIG

RONY PAWAR, MBA

AWARD-WINNING AUTHOR

Size Does Matter – Grow Your Business, Thinking Big

www.sizedoesmatter.biz

Cover design by Azadeh Yaraghi of Gogo Telugo Creatives

Publisher
10-10-10 Publishing
Markham, ON
Canada

Printed in Canada and the United States of America

DEDICATION

This book is lovingly dedicated to my parents **Sukhjit Kaur** and **Daljeet Singh** for supporting me through life's journey.

TABLE OF CONTENTS

Table of Contents

ACKNOWLEDGMENTS

I want to express my gratitude to all those who have encouraged me in one way or another in my life. I also want to convey my thanks to all those who helped me write this book by providing suggestions, brainstorming, allowing me to quote their remarks, and assisting in writing, proof reading, editing, and designing.

Deep thanks go to the **Raymond Aaron Group** for their amazing work in publishing my book. I especially want to thank **Raymond Aaron** for his coaching, writing the foreword, and for presenting me with an award. It's been a true pleasure working with him and learning from him.

One of the best parts of writing a book is acknowledging the wonderful people who have touched my life. My gratitude goes to the following people:

- My utmost respect to my mother **Sukhjit Kaur** and my father **Daljeet Singh** for encouraging me constantly to be a better person throughout my life. My sister **Gursimran** for all her unconditional support and love. My brother **Raminder** for being there for me and the family. My handsome young & energetic nephew **Gurveer** and the cutest helper in my home improvement projects, my little niece **Mehr** for the love and joy they bring in my life everyday.

- I don't have enough words to thank **Azadeh Yaraghi**, the Creative Director and Owner of Gogo Telugo. She is the most magical creative designer & branding expert period. She truly captured the essence of this book and my main concept on the cover design. I also want to thank her for allowing me to use her quote on branding in my book. She holds a very special place in my heart.

- My Cousin **Danny Gill** for his advice and guidance on the subject of operations in the food industry and business in general. His support and mentorship is of huge value in my life.

- **Satbir Minhas**, my BFF and childhood buddy, for keeping me grounded and humble. I am always in awe of him because it seems like the universe took all the wisdom and dumped it into his head. If I ever need authentic advice, I know who to call.

- I want to thank my extended family for all their love and continuous positive influence. My extremely talented and artistic cousins who inspired and encouraged the artist in me while I was growing up **Jyoti, Leena, and Shelly**. The duo brothers **Bawa & Kaki** who were my partners in mischief as kids. **Col Gurbir & Madhu Bhabi, and Harbir** for their encouraging and inspiring words in every conversation. **Beevan & Anupam Kamal** (The Knife Man) for their guidance and mentorship. **Dr. Rajbir & Renu Bhabi** for being the idols I look up to. They are the most loving, kind and genuine human beings I have met. **Danny & Pam** for their huge heart filled with love, support and amazing hospitality each and every time. **Mini & Tony, Neeru & Ajay, Nitu & Gurjit, Paul & Ana, Jyoti, Tina, Shweta & Bali, Ripu,**

Acknowledgments

Kiran, Hatesh, and **Goldy** for the fun, laughter and family support.

- My dear friend **Shami Wadhwa** who influenced me by introducing the idea of getting an MBA in New Zealand, a country that wasn't on my map even in my wildest of the dreams. I thank him for all of his and **Priya's** support in Auckland.

- I want to give a shout out to **Prasann Patel**, my FPG (friend, philosopher & guide) from down under in New Zealand. I can't thank him enough for his mentorship and friendship.

- I would like to thank my buddy **Champak Mehta** for guiding me in my professional journey and for his friendship. Most of all I want to thank him for introducing me to the lifelong lovely friends, the most fun couple **Prasann & Roshni**, the beautiful **Shareen & Thorsk** and one of the most fun and humorous person I have known **Harold Hillman**, who was also huge support in my professional start-up phase in New Zealand.

- My dear friends **Samarvir, Inder, Guree, Vishal, Col Inderpal, Col Sukhbir, Mohan, Anil, Naveen, Bharat, Karam, Darius, Dan & Raghida, Michel & Vanessa J., Ajai, Daria, Patricia, Vanesa & Art, Gautham & Elly, Namalie,** and my dance partners & beautiful friends **Michaela, Alicja, Vanessa G., Sam, Audery,** and **Lauren** for their lifelong friendships and great memories. Huge shout out to my best dance buddy who picked the wrong profession, **Rob Quaresma,** for the great performances together on stage, around the world, and for all the fun times.

- I also want to thank my friends who are no longer physically present but their spirit lives on in sweet memories **Surya, Sameer, Rupinder, Maneesh,** and **Randeep** who taught me the first leadership lesson as a kid.

- My sincere gratitude to **Paul Kalia, CEO Hofmann Plastics Ltd.** and **Dave Baldarelli, COO Meridian Credit Union** for their testimonials. I have a lot of respect for both of them, especially for the common trait that they share in providing inspiration to people around them. I find myself fortunate to have met them.

- My special thanks to **Brigadier Jagdev** and **Brigadier Rawat,** my commanding officers in the Indian Army for grooming me into the leader and officer of one of the most fierce troops in the world, The JATS!

- I learnt a lot from my time in the Indian Military. It's an institution that shaped and influenced my life to a very large extent. The **6th Battalion of The JAT Regiment** family will always be special to me. I'm grateful for the learning and growth during my military career.

- My past professional associates who supported and coached me as well as provided candid feedback for growth: **Lt Col Mavi, Col Dhayal, Brigadier Shekhawat, Col Pandia, James Bradley, Jon Smith, Raj Mitra, Vikram Singh, Dave Baldarelli, Ashutosh Anil, Dave and Greg Feller,** the amazing teams at **Citi, CIBC,** and **Mogo. Annmarie Greer** for giving me my first break in Canada and **June** for giving my first break in New Zealand.

Acknowledgments

- My thanks to **Rob Schock** for giving me the opportunity to assist businesses in Ontario. I would also like to thank the entire team at Business Advisory Services in Ontario Investment Office for their professional advise.

- I want to thank my friend **Karen Di Monte** for introducing me to Raymond Aaron and for giving me the idea of writing a book. Without her this book wouldn't be possible.

- Big thanks to **Suzanne Doyle-Ingram** for her feedback on the book cover and the assistance with the kindle launch of the book. Suzanne's guidance on the publishing process was extremely helpful.

- I appreciate my friend **Cheryl Ivaniski's** motivation during the book writing process.

- I would like to acknowledge **Liz Venttrella** at Raymond Aaron Group for her patience with me especially with all the changes I made to the book. She was fantastic in getting the revisions through and helping me throughout the writing and publishing process.

- Last and not the least, my special thanks to **Tracy Knepple** for her pure magic with the words in helping me put this book together.

FOREWORD

As a business owner or part of senior management, the goal is to have a successful business and navigate the growing pains successfully. In *Size Does Matter: Grow Your Business, Thinking Big*, Rony Pawar provides the guidance needed to make your business thrive and to help you navigate periods of growth successfully.

Rony's experience, both in business consulting and as an officer in the Indian Army, gives him a unique perspective on the challenges and opportunities of leadership in a growing business. Each of the chapters serves a sign post on your journey to building your business successfully. From the practical steps of creating a strategic plan to building up a customer base, Rony focuses on creating an organizational culture focused on growth and achieving milestones for your business.

Right from the start of *Size Does Matter*, Rony answers questions about leadership, marketing, financing, and even the importance of consultants. He also gives you options for research and development that help you get the most out of your investment capital. Rony's wealth of experience also provides you the tools to maintain your organization's financial health through the ups and downs of your industry.

With his real-life examples and his own unique experiences in *Size Does Matter*, Rony illustrates his points in a way that makes sense for any business, regardless of whether you are just starting out or have been in business for years.

This book will be a reference for your business for years to come as you grow your business and your success!

—Raymond Aaron
New York Times Bestselling Author

Introduction

Your business needs to grow. If it doesn't, eventually your business will be out-of-business. Growth is key to the success and longevity, but without the right foundation stones in place, it is not possible. I want to encourage you to view your business with a growth mindset, determining the areas where you need to make changes to create an environment of growth and a thriving business.

What do I mean by a growth mindset? It is a mindset where your focus is on constant improvement, bringing your customers the best experience each and every time. This translates into profitability throughout the life of your business. However, when your business is doing well financially, it can be easy to get into a rut of sorts, if you can keep doing things the same way and continue to achieve the same level of success.

I am here to tell you that is simply not possible. If you don't constantly seek improvement, but just do what has always worked, you will eventually fall behind the competition, and your business will start to suffer as a result. Profits are just one measure of growth, but another is the satisfaction of your customers. Are they returning and recommending your business? Or are you constantly out looking for new customers, because the number of returning customers is limited.

There are several areas that can impact your company's ability to grow. Neglect any of these areas, and the growth simply won't happen. Your business will start to show the signs of that inattention, as you just go through the motions.

This book is meant to be a test of your business. As you read through the following chapters, ask yourself how you personally are doing in these areas. Is your business showing signs of robust growth, or are you noticing a slacking off of growth and profitability?

If you are seeing signs that growth is slowing, then use this book to honestly assess your business and determine where you need to give it some attention. Doing so will help you to keep your business on the robust growth track, avoiding anemic profits and lackluster customer service.

If you are just starting out and opening your first business, then take this book as a guide for how to lay the foundation to explode right out of the gate and keep your company on a growth trajectory. No matter the industry you are in, these principles are timeless keys to growth, and are necessary for any business, no matter what stage it is in.

I am excited to take this journey with you. For many of you, starting your business was about more than just dollars and cents. It was about creating something that would allow you to live the life you have dreamed of, waking up every day to do something that you enjoy and feel passionate about.

It is key to keep your business moving forward to allow you to keep attaining your own personal goals, and keep you excited to go to work every day.

In each chapter of this book, I have laid out critical areas where you need to evaluate the status of your business. Each chapter will discuss one of these critical areas and give you five or six points to access the health of your business and whether it is on the path to growth.

As you read a chapter, ask yourself how your business is operating in this regard. Focus in on the specific steps that you can take to improve in that area. Keep this book close, and refer to it as you work on individual areas. Rome was not built in a day, but by working on each area in this book, you can build your business to be the success you envisioned when you first opened the doors!

Let's burst out of the gate and get motivated to grow!

CHAPTER 1

Leadership & Attitude

As the leader of your business, you set the tone for how your business operates. Your leadership and attitude can influence your business, either to be successful or to eventually fall victim to a lack of growth.

> *"If your actions inspire others to dream more, learn more, do more and become more, you are a leader."*
>
> —John Quincy Adams

So, how do I define a successful leader? After all, you can easily go to the library or local bookstore to pick up hundreds of books on leadership in all areas of your life. But I want to focus on seven main areas of leadership and how they can help you to spur growth in your business, no matter what the industry.

Recognize that leadership does not have to be complicated. It involves tapping into skills you already have, recognizing your vision, using that knowledge to challenge those around you, and then maximizing your skills to achieve your goals!

Strong Leadership

Leadership is such an important element for a business's success that I want to start my book by talking about leadership. Strong and good leadership can transform a poor performing team; however, a poor leadership will definitely bring down a strong performing team. How do you inspire those around you? Are you influencing your team to reach their potential? Is your team following you because they want to or because the corporate structure compels them to?

When you own your business, you are the corporate leadership. You are going to set the tone for how your team will function. The question is, how are you influencing and motivating them to achieve your goals? Are you priming your business for growth or is your team just giving you enough to keep your business afloat?

There is so much written about leadership, and so much debate about whether leaders are born or made. This is what I advise to leaders that I am coaching. You can be whatever you want; it's all in your head. You are always leading someone in your life; most of the time, it's yourself, especially when you motivate yourself to get something done. That's leading *thy self!*

If you are a mom or a dad, then you lead your kids. If you are in a relationship, then you lead your girlfriend or boyfriend, or spouse, and so on and so forth. You have a leader within yourself—it's about channeling that leader and applying the skills necessary to see the results you want.

The skills can be learnt, just like any other skill, or they come with experience. Most of the time, you need a compelling reason to bring out the leader within. When you become parents, the kids compel you to bring out the leader. Moms make great leaders. I have seen them take the lead, including on the dance floor, so many times.

Your employees and customers need to see a strong leader, so they compel you to bring out your own leader from within. People in your business and community will look up to you for vision and direction. If you can't provide that leadership and inspiration, you won't be able to run a successful organization.

You need to be the person that defines the direction of your business, giving them a path to follow. As an entrepreneur, you need to get involved in your business and provide the leadership right from the front, rather than leaving things to your employees. It is important to get in there and lead by example, being willing to get your hands dirty versus just dictating how the jobs should be parceled out.

You are going to set the tone for your business by the type of leader that you are. If your employees can feel your passion, then they are going to get excited about your business, and are going to want to make it successful. But if you treat the business as an afterthought, then they will end up doing the same, as their passion for the business drains away.

What are some keys to strong leadership? You need to be self-confident, have a positive attitude, and the initiative necessary to make everything else fall into place.

I have noticed, over time, that the most successful leaders are the ones willing to get in and get their hands dirty. They are more than just delegators. They want to understand the process and how their workers complete the process daily. You can't understand the challenges your team faces if you don't understand what they have to work with during the course of their job.

I can't help but reflect on some of the different reality shows where the bosses disguise themselves and then go work with their employees. Many come away with a newfound appreciation for what those employees do daily, and how well they do it, despite challenges or inefficiencies.

Strong leaders are also willing to give direction, and set up checkpoints with their employees, but don't micromanage them. I have found that while I want to be aware of what is going on and the potential challenges that could impact the process, I also want to provide guidance and mentorship. Leaders need to be able to trust their teams, while providing support.

How does your team view you? Do they feel your support and encouragement? Can they take your direction, knowing that you truly understand where they are coming from and the challenges they face?

There are going to be members of your team who don't believe they can achieve more. From a leader's perspective, you need to be willing to push them to accomplish more than what they believe is possible. This could mean focusing on training to expand skill sets, finding ways to motivate your team to push the limits, and setting the example by pushing the limits of your own capabilities as well.

You want to help people to achieve the potential that they have, because your business benefits when your employees reach their potential and contribute that to the workplace.

This also applies as the owner of a company when it comes to your top leadership. This could be your CEO, vice-presidents, and key management positions. In the United States, there was a period where top business leaders were leaving President Trump's business councils. The reasons varied from person to person, but as they left, so did that experience and knowledge that they offered to the team.

How are you treating your top leaders? Do you respect their vision and what they bring to your business? Are you maximizing their talents effectively? I will be talking about operations management in Chapter 3, but I want to get you thinking about your top leaders early on. They are the ones that will be on the ground with your teams, and spurring the growth process.

Part of the reason that you need to think about this top leadership is that you want to be creating leaders in your business. You want to build a strong team, with leaders who can step into new roles as your business grows and changes. If you don't address any leadership gaps you may have now, you could find your business struggling to meet the demands of new growth and the forward motion of your industry. You are helping people to lead themselves, creating a path where someone else can pick up where you might have left off.

As a leader, you are providing the map that guides your business on where it is headed. Your vision defines the limits of your business and how you are going to achieve your goals. When you have a strong vision, your employees can feel confident that you are leading them where they need to go to achieve that vision.

A mission statement is one key part of expressing that vision, but you need to make people believe it. Clear communication of your vision, both what your organization stands for and what you are trying to achieve, needs to be done both internally and externally as well.

When your team sees your example, they will be more likely to want to follow you. Strong leadership is key to creating a strong team, willing to work hard and test the boundaries, which is key to growth in any business.

Passion & Inspiration

What are you passionate about? Can other people tell that you are passionate about that topic, or would they be surprised to learn that about you?

When you talk about your business, your team needs to feel your passion for the business. They need to see you excited and motivated to reach the goals of the business, and then set even more. Not every member of your team is going to be motivated the same way.

I worked with one client who had a team manager that wasn't really engaged and doing what they felt he could be doing to increase the team's performance. As a result, this manager's team was consistently in 7th or 8th place, quarter after quarter. I found out that he was working to pay bills and save to start his own business. He wasn't interested in helping this business grow, because he was focused on his own goals. My advice was to show him that he could be learning skills to help him run his own business as he was working in his current managerial position.

The questions I asked were focused on understanding his motivation and how the company could leverage that to get the best out of him as part of the team. We were able to point out that if he couldn't make this team successful, then he was unlikely to be able to make his own business successful, because he hadn't built up his skill set to do so. When we got him to change his point of view, recognizing that he was learning skills necessary for his business, but not on his dime, we were able to motivate him to learn what was necessary to lead and manage his own business.

In two months, that team came to the top of the list. The next quarter, his team was in the number one slot. He didn't work there forever, but while he did, his team was consistently performing at the top.

As a business owner, you don't need to have all the skills. You can hire the people with the skills you need. If you are looking for a business plan or accounting skills, you can find individuals to fill these roles. The most important skill you need to develop is motivating and inspiring people. You can't delegate this task to someone else. It is your responsibility. Growth can't happen if your team is only doing enough to get by. They need to be inspired to see how the company's goals can impact their own.

Your own efforts on behalf of your business can provide that motivation or can work against you. Does the team see you actively working toward your goals? Do they see you living and breathing your mission statement? Or are you setting a tone of just getting by? Your employees will reach for the bar you set, but only if they can see your efforts, passion, and willingness to work hard to achieve growth.

Find what inspires your team, and then use that to motivate them to reach new heights. It is important to use *carrots* to get the best from your team, instead of constantly using fear of the consequences, to achieve results. When you have an inspired and motivated team, the possibilities of growth and success are endless.

> *"Your attitude, not your aptitude, will determine your altitude."*
>
> —Zig Ziglar

Having a Winning Attitude—It's Infectious

Have you ever spent time with someone who was positive, excited about the possibilities, and was determined to reach their goals? It was infectious and probably made you start looking at thinking differently yourself. You got excited, because they were excited.

Your team functions in much the same way. If you lead with a negative attitude, then your team isn't going to be positive and look for ways to grow and move the business forward. They are likely to assume failure is the outcome, and achieve to meet that outcome.

Here is the point when you need to really do a heartfelt examination of your own attitude at work and in front of your team. You need to understand how your attitude is impacting them, and the environment being created as a result.

I am a firm believer that attitude is the key. If the leader doesn't have the right attitude, it won't flow down the chain and reflect in the rest of the organization. For example, if Steve Jobs didn't have the attitude that he wanted to create something completely different and revolutionary when he created the iPhone and the iPad, then his team wouldn't have kept those designs coming until he found the one that became the one button design we all know so well.

It was an attitude that demanded excellence. You will get what you demand. If you demand success, then that is what you will get. If you accept mediocrity from your team, then that is what you will get. Your attitude as a leader will define your team, and they will meet the bar you set based on what you are willing to accept.

I served in the military back in India, and I was leading an anti-terrorist operation at one point in my career. Being part of these types of operations is truly a game of cat and mouse. You must do some things covertly, and you might not always get the right intel. There were challenges. But my attitude was that we had to do whatever it took to get these guys. I pushed my team to the limit, expecting their best as we did our work. Once we tasted success, however, individuals who weren't even a part of my team were approaching me about joining the team. They wanted to be part of the winning team. Your attitude is infectious but also your success. People want to be successful, and they look to be part of teams achieving that success.

Your team will help your business to grow, especially if you provide them a taste of success. They will be motivated to go after the growth opportunities because they will want to be part of a winning team. Does your attitude project a sense of excitement and determination to win? If so, then your team will benefit from your attitude. Choosing the right attitude will translate into success, because your skill set is only one part of your leadership. Attitude is another, but without action, neither of these things will result in the growth necessary for your business.

Getting Things Done

Good leadership is about getting things done and creating tangible results. For a team, the abstract isn't going to be good enough. You can think and plan all day long, but if you don't execute, then you haven't accomplished anything.

If you are a thinker, who is always planning, but you don't create the right environment to execute, then you won't see the growth you need. How do you create that environment? It starts with having the right management team in place and then leading them to meet your goals for the business. This is where the rubber hits the road. All the parts of leadership become key at this point because this is where you implement them to reap the rewards.

It is very important to a company to get their products completed on a specific timeline, and out into the marketplace, because that is what will ensure their success. Creating a plan, but not executing it, will never get the results you want for your business. As a leader, it becomes your job to hold the owners accountable, to make sure that everything has been properly delegated, that you have the necessary pieces to meet your timeline, and that you have the right resources in place and are keeping on the timeline to meet the milestones. Additionally, once you have reached the milestones, it is important to debrief your team and find out what worked and what didn't.

If there were sources of frustration, or places where the communication didn't move effectively, then you need to adjust, as the leader, to correct those areas. Feedback is key, but if you do nothing with the feedback, then it becomes useless to your company. Action is critical to the growth of your company in all areas.

Communication is the Key

No matter what type of organization you have, being a leader means being able to clearly define your message for your team. Communication starts from the top down. If your message isn't clear to your team, then you will find yourself leading a team that isn't performing.

I have seen leadership have a clear idea of where they want their company to go, but by not making that clear to the team, each member tries to fulfill the goals of the team their own way, and as a result, confusion reigns. Energy is wasted and the team flounders. Have you noticed your team struggling to move forward? Do they seem to lack a cohesive goal or strategy for getting there?

If so, then you need to look at how you are communicating with your team. If you have a plan that no one is executing, then it could be because you aren't clearly communicating the actions necessary as part of the plan. Your team needs to understand their part in the bigger picture, but it also helps to have an idea of what the bigger picture is!

Leadership needs to set the right tone, and they need to communicate the mission and vision of the company, what the goals are, where you are going, what you want to achieve, and how you are going to achieve it. Most organizations have goals and milestones set to define their progress, but they don't communicate what the aim is behind the goals that were set, or how each employee contributes to those goals. The team will then struggle to meet those goals.

Unless the employees relate to the goals, and understand the mission of the organization, they may struggle to get behind the company and give their best efforts. If you are a front-line employee, but you don't see any line of sight between your job and the organization's success, then you will feel like another drop in the ocean. Organizations that make their employees a priority will have productive and satisfied employees, but if you treat your employees as cogs in the wheels of your organization, then they will not give you their very best.

High level engagement with their employees is a marker of the success of an organization, and starts with the leadership. Here is a wonderful example of this in the story of a visit by President Kennedy to NASA. He had set the goal of the U.S. putting a man on the moon. On this visit, he met a janitor and asked him what his purpose was at NASA. The janitor replied that he was helping to put a man on the moon.

That was a case of the message being clearly communicated to the team, and they all understood how their contributions made the successful achievement of that goal possible. He wasn't a scientist or a manager or anything, but he understood how his work contributed to the goal.

Respect & Integrity

As part of communication, recognize that good communication is evidence of the respect you have for your employees. As a leader, it is important to have people look up to you and see that you walk the talk, demonstrating integrity and fairness to your employees.

If you are demonstrating these qualities as a leader, then you can ask for the same from your employees. But if you are not showing integrity in the way you do business, you can't demand it from your employees. It is not just something you do but needs to be a part of who you are, and something that flows from your professional life to your personal one.

Both inside and outside your company, you need to be someone who keeps their word and delivers as promised. If you don't do that, then you can't expect your employees to do it for you. As a leader, you set the tone for your company, which ultimately creates your company's reputation within the community and your industry.

When you hear about a company's employees who were not performing their jobs with integrity, it reflects poorly on the company as a whole. Employees follow the leadership of the company and the standards they set. If you, as the leader, are not setting and maintaining high standards for yourself, then your team will not expect to be held to a higher standard.

Yet this is where many leaders fail their teams. They expect great things, and set high standards, but are not willing to meet them as a leader. The team ultimately begins to question why they are working so hard to meet the standards that the leadership is unwilling to meet. When your team questions why they are working so hard, you will start to see productivity suffer. The best leaders, be it in business or parenting, lead by example, not by a *"do as I say, not as I do"* attitude. If growth is your aim, then your leadership needs to reflect the standards of your business. It starts with you!

If you don't talk about integrity and respect with your team, then they will be less likely to demonstrate it among the members of the team, or to your customers and clients.

Ask yourself how you are doing in this area. Do you find yourself willing to accept less than the best from yourself? Is that attitude trickling down to your team? Or are you showing your team little respect, yet demanding respect from them? How is that impacting the productivity and goals of the organization?

It is important to take the time to examine how you are doing in this regard. Much of what you hope to achieve as a leader starts with your attitude and how you treat others— both your team and your clients. When you see yourself demonstrating integrity and clamping down on activities that are counter to that standard, then you will see your organization take large steps toward the growth that you want for your business.

This isn't just limited to the people in your organization but the processes and products that you put out. Are you willing to accept sub-standard work, as long as you don't get caught? Your people will see that and think it is acceptable. You can't have two sets of standards but must be clear and consistent in following one particular set of standards for your business. It can't be a case of *say one thing, but do another*. Why? Because of the impact it will have on your brand.

Social Responsibility and Community Engagement

If you are demonstrating integrity, and setting the example for your organization, then you will reap the rewards in terms of creating a brand that the community can trust. But if your employees think it is okay to cut corners, then this can have a huge impact on your brand and its reputation. Unhappy customers tell others, and you will find it harder to maintain your share of the market.

Volkswagen is a great example of this. The company was caught lying about the level of the emissions their cars produced. Now, I don't know if this was a conscious decision by the leadership of the organization, but someone, somewhere, got the idea that this would be acceptable to do. However, the impact to its brand as this story unfolds, and to the organization, is huge.

Their reputation within the community has been tainted, and it will make it hard for them to build trust with the consumer again. Their integrity has been tainted, and the buck stops with the top guy. The leader is always the one who is going to be held accountable for these types of situations, so it is important to keep the message of the organization consistently focused on integrity. It is your job to make sure that your company is acting with integrity.

Social responsibility, and engagement with your community, involves more than just your integrity, but that is a key part of building your brand.

Today, social media and the internet has made it possible to share information with just a click of the button. One doesn't need to wait for regulators to come and audit your company to know when something is not right. There is more to your social reputation, however, than being compliant with regulations. Are you environmentally friendly? Are you doing the types of things that make your company a good neighbor to those communities around you?

Are you giving back to your community? Are you sponsoring charity events and support causes throughout the community? Various organizations have created a line in their budgets geared toward helping and supporting their community. In doing so, they also encourage their employees to be more engaged with the local causes of their community.

Today, individuals want to work with companies that are worried about more than just the bottom line. They want to be engaged with companies that are concerned about their impact on the community they call home. Demonstrate that you care about the community, and your clients will reward your loyalty to their community, with loyalty to your brand or business. Be an active partner in your community, and you will create a win-win situation for your business.

Community engagement means that you are helping your employees to see the impact of what they do, on their community. Job satisfaction can increase when they can see the real-world results of their efforts. As a leader, you are contributing because it is the right thing to do, but also because it is good for your company to be a good neighbor, wherever you call home.

Throughout this chapter, I have focused on several key areas where a leader needs to be active to see successful growth from their team and their company. But this is just the beginning. As you will soon see, you also need to have more than the right attitude and good communication skills.

You need a plan to move your company forward, with a map that defines the direction your company will need to go in the future. Strategic planning is part of your company's growth. I get excited when I work with business owners who are excited about defining where their companies are headed. How do you define your company's path? I can't wait to explore that with you in the next chapter.

CHAPTER 2
Strategic Planning

As the leader of your organization, you are growing your leadership skills, which is admirable. But even the best leaders can struggle when they aren't clear where the business is headed. Having a strategic plan is key to moving your business to the next level of growth.

A great leader can only be truly effective if they know the direction the business is headed. This chapter, and the next, will be key to growing your business—the real meat and potatoes of taking your business to the next level. Take the time to look at how your business is doing in each of these areas. Jot down what could stand to be improved. As you will see, knowing where you want to go is important, but you also need to have a plan to get there and the resources to execute effectively.

Where do you want to take your business? You might have some goals, but without a set of processes and a plan to execute them, reaching those goals and creating explosive growth will be difficult.

Vision and Mission of Your Organization

Your business is similar to a ship. Without the right guidance system in place, you aren't going to end up reaching your destination, no matter how many times you turn the wheel or the effort you put into steering the ship.

Your business is going to operate just like that ship. You need to have a defined destination and the right guidance to reach that destination in order to be successful. This is where the vision and mission of your organization is key.

Vision—the ability to think about or plan the future with imagination or wisdom

As I meet various business owners, CEOs, and CFOs, I find that there is a disconnect from what they think and where they are guiding the organization. They are entrepreneurs, and they are passionate about their business, but they are all over the map regarding how to move to the next level. Their passion gets their team excited, but the lack of direction can also leave their teams feeling frustrated.

Mission—a strongly felt aim, ambition, or calling

These leaders haven't defined the vision and the mission of their business. Vision defines what your organization stands for, while the mission of your business defines why it exists. A business leader needs to know what the vision and mission of their organization is, but also needs to be able to clearly communicate that to their team, vendors, and clients of their business.

People often confuse these two. When I am working with clients, I will take the Google definitions and outline how each of these works regarding their business. Then I will challenge them to outline their vision. This can often help them to transform their vision into the mission statement of their business.

Your mission statement doesn't need to be long, drawn-out,

and full of flowery phrases. Instead, it needs to be a few sentences, typically two or three, using clear and concise language to define your mission.

Your business, however, may have started out with a clear mission and vision of where you were headed. But has that continued to be accurate in the face of changes to your industry and your business as a whole? Often, you can get so involved in running your business, you can lose sight of why you got into the business in the first place.

Therefore, it is so important to spend time on the strategic process and planning stages. You don't know what you don't know. Some may find strategic planning as a waste of time, or may not even realize that they need to do it. I am here to tell you that strategic planning is key to the growth and success of your business. You are not going to see your business reach its potential without strategic planning.

Now, let me ask you this. On your last vacation, did you know where you were going? Did you create a plan to arrive at your destination, and perhaps even plan some activities for key points in the trip? Doing so, likely contributed to how enjoyable the trip was but also how much you appreciated the vacation afterwards. While most of us would not dream of going on vacation without planning the trip and all the details, too many business owners don't spend that same effort on strategic planning for their business.

I advise my clients to take time annually to do strategic planning, both for the year and for checking in on long-term future goals. Are you getting close to reaching some of them? Have you set new goals to replace them? Ideally, the best time to review your strategic plan is at the beginning of your fiscal year. You can use this time to see where you are headed but also to define the resources available, and allocate them to reach your goals for the year.

This is the time to do a reality check. If you set goals last year, did you meet them? If not, why not? What are your goals for this year? Are there specific steps you need to take to reach them? Is your team aware of these goals and how they can contribute to your business reaching them?

Your vision and mission are the first steps on the path of strategic planning. But it involves more than just an idea of where you are going; it involves a defined plan to reach your destination and achieve your goals.

Strategy Roadmap

Have you ever gone on a trip to somewhere you have never been, without a map? Today, most of us have an app on our phones or tablets, which will give us directions, but it still provides guidance to help us reach our destination.

Your business will also benefit from having a map showing you how to get where you want to go. Too many businesses flounder because, even though they may have a clear mission, they aren't clear on how they are going to reach their destination. Thus, they are driving around, occasionally recognizing a few key landmarks, but they are unlikely to reach their destination.

To achieve your vision and be able to live the mission of your business, you need to know how you are going to get there. It is about getting from your current state to your desired state. Your mission statement is a high-level overview of where you want to go, but your strategy roadmap is all about nailing down the details. It needs to be specific, and clearly lay out how you are going to get from your current state to your desired state.

For example, let's go back to your vacation. You have a destination in mind; maybe in Europe, or some other country that you have never been to before. But you are in Canada, or the United States. How are you going to get to your desired location? You might start by looking at flights, determining the cost of those flights and other details of the trip, and then setting up a budget, so that you can save the funds necessary. You wouldn't just show up at the airport and expect to get a seat on a flight to your desired location. It would take planning and effort to reach your destination.

Your business is going to achieve the growth you plan for, not the growth you hope for.

To start out, you need to define your larger goals. Then, you need to break down those goals into milestones. What are your short-term, middle-term, and long-term milestones that can help you determine whether you are reaching your goals? This will help you to define the best strategy for your business to meet its goals of growth, while still providing stability.

It is important to build this roadmap in order to be able to hold yourself, and your organization, accountable for meeting those milestones, and to put stakeholders in place to divide responsibilities, as well as be the guide to help you budget your resources. This is the key to the success of your organization. Without it, you are sailing in the ocean and following the current, instead of setting a course and defining where you are headed.

How does your roadmap help you to stay on track? On a quarterly basis, or more frequently, depending on the milestones you have set, you can check in and determine if you are meeting your milestones. If you are not meeting them, this is the time to determine why, before you lose a whole year or more, essentially making no progress toward achieving your defined goals.

However, these checks throughout the year can help you to make course corrections that greatly impact your ability to reach your milestones and achieve your goals for your business. Without them, you will be rudderless and, in today's marketplace, no business can maintain any level of success, let alone grow, without a strategic roadmap in place.

Organizational Structure

Part of creating your roadmap means assigning individuals to complete various tasks that will move the organization forward and help them to achieve the milestones you have set for your business. However, that type of accountability will only be successful if you make sure that you have the right people in place, and that you are actively supporting them with training and the right infrastructure.

You need to have an organizational structure in place that will support your strategic roadmap. For example, you might want to upgrade the technology within your operations. You need to be sure that you have the right structure in place for this type of upgrade. This means that you might need to bring in new personnel, with specific skill sets, to increase the technology savvy of your organization.

If you are building a house, you need to make sure the foundation is sound. Your organization's foundation is the people that provide the framework for your business. If you do not put the right people in the right positions, you run the risk of being unable to support the plans of your strategic roadmap, because you lack the skills needed to get yourself to the next level.

Once you have your strategy, you will be able to determine the type of structure that you will need for your business. If you are building a house, you wouldn't order supplies before going to an architect to determine what the structure will look like and what will be needed. Why would you hire individuals for key positions before you determine what those key positions will be?

As you build your strategic roadmap, look at your current employees. Are there skills that you are not tapping into? Could certain individuals be more effective in a different position within your organization?

I want you to start thinking about how your business is functioning right now. As you do so, you might find key areas where skills sets are lacking, or even whole departments that need to be reorganized or created. Be willing to make the investments in your organizational structure, because doing so will help you to maximize the effectiveness of your strategic roadmap, and help you to reach your goals of growth even sooner.

SWOT Analysis

As part of the analysis of your organization, you will need to find out a few key pieces of knowledge, as outlined below:

- **S**—Strengths
- **W**—Weaknesses
- **O**—Opportunities
- **T**—Threats

Each of these areas will reveal something you need to understand about your business and the people working in it. Doing a SWOT analysis of your organization means determining where your organization stands in these key areas. You are doing an internal analysis so you can understand where you stand as a business.

Your mission may have lofty goals, and you may have a strategic roadmap in place, but that doesn't mean that your business is ready to start tackling all those lofty goals. It might mean that you need to have some pre-milestones, with a focus on getting your business ready to focus on those lofty goals. A SWOT analysis is an in-depth way of accessing your business objectively, and making the improvements needed to obtain growth in the next quarter, in the next year, and in the next five years.

As part of the process, understand that you will be building on your strengths, and making changes to address your weaknesses. However, don't think that this is an analysis that can be done once and never done again. It needs to be a regular part of your routine to constantly understand where your company is right now.

For instance, you might have isolated a weakness in your organizational structure. But without a regular SWOT analysis, you may find it easy to put off addressing that weakness, which could make it worse in the long run. Yet, with a regular routine of analysis and accountability, those weaknesses can be identified and addressed, and new ones can be uncovered.

Let's face it. No business reaches a point where they can say, "We are perfect. We are performing at an optimal level and nothing more needs to be done." It simply isn't possible. Technology changes, industries change, and employees may leave. Additionally, not every business knows what their weaknesses are or what opportunities might be available for them. You may have an idea, but you might not have tracked them to determine if those are actual weaknesses or real opportunities.

Threats could come from competition or your business not having the right tools at the right time. Global trade agreements could also impact your business, creating threats from the macro-environment. Internally, you could find that you aren't keeping up with your industry and its changes, which means you face the threat of being obsolete. However, if you don't take the time to identify these threats, you can't make the necessary changes in your business to adjust and counter them.

A SWOT analysis, done annually, is so important because, if you don't know where you stand, you can't make the necessary adjustments to help your business thrive within a changing economic landscape. New information will be available every year, as you make changes due to altering circumstances or new information.

Without knowledge of where your business is, you also can't adjust your roadmap, and you can't expect to create sustainable growth. It simply won't be possible.

Macro-environment & Competitor Awareness

Completing a SWOT analysis, and understanding your macro-environment, along with being aware of your competitors, goes hand in hand. A macro-environment analysis means understanding what is going on in the marketplace and in your industry. There are plenty of factors that can impact your business, but again, if you aren't aware of them, you can adjust and prepare for them.

Dynamics within the larger global marketplace can also impact your business, as changes to trade agreements or diplomatic relations could impact your ability to import necessary supplies, or export your products.

Additionally, it is key to understand who your competition is, and what are they doing within the marketplace. Are they creating big changes that are grabbing them more of a market share? How are they setting the pace, or are they adjusting to keep up with your business? As industries change, and the economic landscape adjusts to new technology, your business may go from driving your industry, to being part of the pack. You also need to be aware of how technology is impacting your industry.

Technology and its lightning fast changes mean that one way of doing business could quickly become obsolete. Customers who don't see you making efforts to adapt to industry changes may see you as a less viable partner over time. If you aren't keeping up as a business, then you could make yourself obsolete.

That is why these analyses are so critical. Without them, you can find yourself caught unaware, and your business could be greatly impacted by outside forces. Your strategic roadmap is meant to help you take the ideal future and make it a reality, but if you aren't aware of what is going on around your business, you could be setting goals that are unattainable in the face of larger industry changes.

While you might not be able to do something to address everything out there, you need to be aware, because it is impacting your business in one form or another. Now that you have done all these analyses, and have your hand on the pulse of your business, I want you to start thinking about implementing change in a measurable way.

Goals & Targets

Have you ever had a specific physical goal that you wanted to achieve? It could be anything from losing weight to competing in a marathon. Part of your efforts to achieve your goal could include more physical exercise, strength training, and changes to your diet. But how would you know if any of your efforts have been successful?

You would need to measure certain areas to determine if you were reaching your target. For weight loss, you might weigh yourself once a week, with an expectation that the number would be going down. For a marathon, you might measure how quickly you can cover a mile, with the expectation that your time will continue to get shorter.

If those expectations were not met, you might re-evaluate what you are doing, and make changes, because your current actions aren't helping you to successfully achieve your goal. It is no different in your business.

You might have identified weaknesses or opportunities that you want to address. Yet, without creating measurable metrics, you can't determine if your changes are having the right impact. Without goals and targets, your strategic roadmap and your analyses are just pieces of paper.

These are key to making your business goals tangible. They break down your strategy roadmap even further, giving you measurable metrics to use to determine your progress to your goals.

However, I want to caution you that doing your analyses could bring a lot of potential adjustments to the forefront. You might want to deal with them all but find yourself overwhelmed by what that would mean in terms of time and capital.

This is where doing annual analyses becomes key. You can create short-term goals to address immediate concerns, mid-term goals to address things that you see having a greater impact in the future, and long-term goals for the vision you have of your company. Understand that your short-term and mid-term goals will be addressing specific issues, but they should ultimately help to move your business closer to achieving your long-term goals.

Goals and targets can hold you accountable to achieving specific outcomes in your business, in terms of sales or other areas you want to address. Metrics can help you to determine if you are on target to meet your goals or if you need to make further changes. Using metrics, you can also determine if you have met a goal, and whether it is time to create a new one to replace it. No analysis of your business should be without tangible metrics to track.

One area I want to address is that of striving to meet your goals versus just trying to meet your goals. Using stretch goals, you can empower your team to achieve more than just the goals that you set. For example, if your goal is $1 million in sales, then consider setting a stretch goal of $2 million. You are more likely to reach the $1 million goal as a result. However, without that stretch goal, you are less likely to reach your $1 million goal.

Another way to look at it is the *Meet, Exceed,* and *Exceptional.*

The minimum goal is your *Meet,* and then there should be other targets (*Exceed* and *Exceptional*) that are slightly outside of your comfort zone. Those goals will require that you stretch yourself beyond what you are already comfortable achieving.

When you are setting incentive goals for your teams, set these stretch goals, and give incentives for reaching them. Then, you will get what you need, while motivating them to exceed your expectations.

Additionally, you need to break down your short-term goals into daily, weekly, and monthly targets. These will help you to build momentum as you strive to reach those mid-term and long-term goals. Benchmarks give you the ability to track how you are doing in terms of your historical metrics, your competition, and your own internal goals and targets.

This type of measuring will also dovetail nicely into your forecast, allowing you to make achievable goals for the upcoming year, as part of your planning process.

Measure of Success at Each Level of the Organization

One of the keys of measuring success is directly related to the targets that you have set. For example, you have set a goal of making $12 million in sales for a year, which breaks down to $1 million per month. As you get a couple of months into the year, you can check to see if you are reaching that monthly target. Keep in mind, most businesses have months where they reach their targets, and other months where they fall short. Averaging this out will give you a run rate, which can help you to determine if you are on track or if your team is falling behind.

I also want to point out that you need to be tracking the success of all the levels of your organization. It can be very easy to set specific goals for the entire company without going any deeper.

But these goals can mean different things to various levels of your organization. Each of their targets will contribute to the larger goal. If you are creating accountability within your organization, then you need to make sure they understand what they are accountable for.

A unit of your company might be dependent on another unit to complete their tasks, before that unit can move forward to meeting its deliverables. Are you aware of the synergy of the various levels of your company? Do you find that bottlenecks come back to specific levels of your organization repeatedly? It could mean that you need to make changes in various processes to allow all the levels of your organization to be successful.

What tends to happen most often in organizations is that goals are set at a very high level or just for the front-line staff. As a result, the rest of the organization might lack any metrics to judge their own progress. How can you make sure all the levels of your organization have their specific goals that reflect what they contribute?

Start by taking the large organizational goal and breaking it down level by level. As you do so, you can assign targets to individual departments and their leadership. This can also help you to better understand how the various levels of your organization interact with each other to reach these targets.

Goals can be set down to the individual level; however, a word of caution: if you can't measure a goal, don't have it as a goal. If it is going to be subjective and up in the air, then no one can fairly meet the expectations of that goal. Make sure you can measure your goals effectively because, if not, you could be wasting time and resources to achieve an unattainable goal or target.

With that in mind, you need to know what your key performance indicators (KPIs) are, and have a way of tracking them. One of these is the leading indicators, which basically lead up to or provide an understanding of how the business is trending in its performance. Leading indicators are not necessarily performance indicators, so they might not be a quality measurement of specific targets, but they can be used to get an idea of the big picture and what's coming down the road.

Performance indicators give you very specific details about how a certain team or individual is doing in terms of reaching their goals and targets. They can also be used to determine if an individual qualifies for various incentives.

Take, for example, a car dealership. You might have set a specific target of selling 40 cars in a month. With four salespeople, that breaks down to a goal of 10 cars per salesperson. Halfway through the month, you may have only sold 10 cars total. While performance indicators will give you the specifics of how each salesperson is performing, a leading indicator could be how many appointments are being set with potential buyers. If you want to sell 40 cars in a month, but only have 20 appointments set, then even though you have already sold 10 cars, you are unlikely to reach your monthly target based on a 20% closing rate.

That leading indicator, therefore, can be a great way to make changes mid-stream to affect the outcome. As the owner of that dealership, you might push to get more appointments set, thus increasing the likelihood of reaching your goal of selling 40 cars that month. How are you trending, and what changes can you make to reach your goals, instead of flying blind throughout the month?

Tracking success helps you to define the success of your organization. What you make as a daily, weekly, and monthly target will define what daily, weekly, and monthly success looks like.

Additionally, depending on the level of the organization and your department, success will be different. Using various tracking tools, you can motivate your employees because they can see how they are progressing, the difference they are making, and how successful they are going to be as individuals.

The question is, where does all this information come from?

Big Data

Organizations have a lot of data, numbers, and information that is available for you to tap into, or not. All the activities that happen within your organization are generally being recorded somewhere and in some type of fashion.

Take Google and their glasses for a moment. They sent out individuals to malls and shopping centers, wearing these glasses. Everything those individuals looked at or touched became big data. Once you do something with that data, it becomes information.

You apply intelligence to that data, and you turn it into something tangible that you can work with to create change. However, depending on what data you capture, you could be missing out on some key indicators on the health and wellness of your business. However, once you capture it, you need to be able to turn it into something that will help your business to grow and succeed.

Depending on the size of the organization, there might also be a whole lot of industrial data available as well. Think about Facebook and Google. They are collecting data constantly, but transforming it can help you to capture this data and turn it into something that allows you to make data-driven decisions versus anecdotal ones. You need to make decisions that are supported by facts. Data can provide those facts to help you to define your next course of action based on the nature of your business. This data and facts can also help you to define your goals for your strategic roadmap based on what you want to achieve in the future, and if those goals are sustainable.

According to Danny Singh, Vice-President of Operations at

Marcos Pizza, "If we don't have data, then we won't know what to expect."

What this means at store level, at Marcos, is being able to analyze and determine when your busiest times are, and then staff or have the necessary products in advance of those busy times. The data-driven decisions can help you to address those periods of slow sales as well. The question may be, "How can I present this to my team without overwhelming them?"

Visual Analytics

Visual analytics are a way to make the data palatable for your audience, be it your team or other members of the leadership of your organization. Creating pictures, such as grafts and pie charts, can convey information quickly, in a way that allows for a plan to be created, without devoting a ton of time to the issues of sitting down and sifting through spreadsheets of numbers to determine the trend and what needs to be done.

The point of analyzing all this data is to find the best ways to put it to good use for your company. But you don't want to be devoting so much of your team's operational resources to analysis that they have little time for implementation or other necessary tasks in the daily running of your business.

Remember when I talked about finding the skills you need for your business? This is one of those cases. Finding a good analyst is key to freeing up resources in other areas of your business, so they can implement your strategies based on what you learn from your data. Using an analyst, you can find the nuggets that are valuable for your team and put them into a form that allows someone to understand them quickly and act effectively.

You need to remember that you want to keep your business moving, but you don't want to be tying up your operational teams with trying to figure out what all the data you have collected means for them. Make it easy to digest, and it will help to contribute to the growth of your company.

At this point, however, I want to caution you against over-analyzing your data to the point that you paralyze your company by not making any decisions at all. The data is going to give you multiple options and plenty of things to measure. But you aren't going to be able to tackle everything. The point is to choose the most critical decisions to make, based on timing. It is a fine line between analytics and decision-making.

Therefore, choose the key areas in which you want to focus. It should be based on your strategic goals for the year. Every year, you may find the need to change that focus slightly to address a weakness, an opportunity, or a threat.

If you aren't willing to spend the time on strategic planning, you are going to end up spinning the wheels of your business. You won't make any progress in growing and building your business. If you want to grow, then you need to make sure that these are the areas you focus on initially.

Now that you have an idea of where you want to take your business, it is time to focus on operating it in a way that will help you to reach your strategic goals. Turn your attention to the next chapter, where I am going to guide you through what operations management is, and how it can be pivotal to growing your business to the next level.

CHAPTER 3

Operations Management

The beauty of a strategic plan is that it helps you to define where you are going, but without the right operations in place, that plan will remain a document on the shelf of your business. Now that you have your plan, let's address how to make it possible to achieve it by means of your operations.

What do I mean by operations? It is simply all the areas of your business that allow it to function, especially if you are producing a product or providing a specific service. Throughout this chapter, I want to focus on your employees and your team as a whole. In thinking about your team, you might be focused on how many sales they have produced, or how well they built a product or delivered a service to keep a customer coming back.

Instead, for now, I want you to focus on how they are interacting with you and each other, as well as the skills that they bring to your business. The point of this chapter is to not only keep your organization operating at peak levels but to also make sure that your employees are invested in the success of your business. When they are, then growth will happen, even faster than you might expect!

Your employees have different needs. Each of them will impact their performance at work, but it is important to understand how your company's culture can impact each of these areas. Let's look at Maslow's hierarchy of need. The first is physiological, the second is safety, but the third is love and belonging. Here are how those other areas can be associated with the work environment.

- Physiological—The need to have food/shelter, essentially a place to work that provides a paycheck to care for those needs.

- Safety—The need to have a safe work environment, where they can be productive without fear of harm.

- Love/Belonging—Feeling wanted, a sense of belonging, and to be part of a team.

- Esteem—To feel respected and valued in the workplace.

- Self-actualization—Intellectually challenged, reaching targets, and understanding the impact of their skills and experience.

The culture of your business needs to be welcoming to your employees, making them feel as if they belong. Recognition and a reward system are a way to achieve that sense of belonging, because you are acknowledging their contribution to your company, and how their efforts are key to the company's success and growth.

Employee Engagement

As a business leader, you need to make sure that your employees are engaged in the business—not just because you want them to be productive—you need them to feel emotionally invested in the business, as if they owned a part of it. They need to understand how they benefit from their efforts as part of the team, instead of feeling as if the leadership is the only beneficiary of their hard work.

When an employee takes personal ownership in the results of their company, they will also hold themselves to a higher standard and give a better effort than an employee who is just there to do enough to collect their check and go home. You need to create a sense of belonging among your employees. They are part of the business, and they need to feel that connection, which is key to building or maintaining their level of job satisfaction.

You want to build a culture where people want to come to work. In one instance, I was working with a company where the sick calls were high on Fridays; people wanted to enjoy a long weekend, but that meant productivity went down on Fridays. The question was how to make people want to come to work on Friday, instead of wanting to call in sick.

Now, as a company, you could get punitive, but that is unlikely to endear your team to your company. They may come in to avoid the penalty, but they are not going to be motivated to be any more productive.

The point is to make the work environment compelling to get the employees to come into work and be productive. To overcome this challenge, we started potluck Fridays. Everyone brought in a different dish, and there was a theme for each potluck Friday. The result was *Theme Days,* where we would choose to focus on a different type of food, and then they added dress-up. People started coming in on their days off because it was so much fun.

Attendance improved on Fridays to 100%. It created a culture that got the employees wanting to come to work and to get engaged while they were there. Look at your company. Are there specific times where the productivity appears to go down? Are you noticing a lack of engagement? Perhaps you need to change the routine to get individuals excited again about the work they are doing.

Recognition is also important to job satisfaction. It doesn't need to break the bank, but simple rewards for a job well-done can go a long way with your employees. For your employees, there are needs that must be met, as described in Maslow's hierarchy of needs, which I discussed earlier. When your corporate culture takes the time to do so, the team benefits. Let's talk about the various aspects of your productivity and processes, as well as how your corporate culture and the engagement of your team can impact each of these areas.

Productivity

As a business, efficient operations can make or break a business. This is where everything happens in your business. Everything else is in support of your operations. Productivity is focused on how you are running your day-to-day operations. How are products and services moving from point A to point B, and in how much time, and what is the quality of the output?

If you are a manufacturing company, for example, how efficient is your production environment? Are your processes allowing your employees to reach their optimal performance, or are there areas that need to be addressed to improve efficiency, without sacrificing quality?

How many shifts are you running? Are you utilizing your capacity fully, in terms of your machinery and the production time of your people?

One of the biggest areas that contributes to low productivity is downtime. This is the time that your employees and machines are available to work, but for whatever reason, they aren't producing anything. In a contact center, if you have 100 people working, but there are no calls coming in, then you aren't being productive. This is just one example of downtime, but there are many others. Think about areas where you could automate your production, reducing the amount of downtime.

You need to execute on your strategic plans to achieve your goals and targets. This is the meat and potatoes of the business, and where the rubber hits the road. You have created an amazing plan for the growth of your business, but now you need to execute to see that plan come to fruition, and to achieve those growth goals that you set for your business.

You need to be supporting your production environment through training, processes, and other functional areas to achieve what you want out of your business. However, if you are unwilling to allow others to take on parts of the process and use their skills, you will become the bottleneck to your business as you try to micro-manage your productivity. Let's talk about what delegation really means and why it is such an art for those leaders who do it well.

Art of Delegation

There is a reason why I call this the art of delegation. It is a very subtle balance and a judgment call on how much you can delegate, who you can delegate to, and what you can delegate. Many leaders can get stuck in this area and find themselves worn out as they take on more than they need to, when others could be used to complete those tasks.

As a business owner, you do need to maintain control and oversight on your business, but at the same time, you don't want to be the one who makes every decision throughout the day. However, you don't want to take away your ability to know what is going on, even if you aren't always involved in all day-to-day activities that you have delegated to others.

For example, an executive might have his administrative

assistant handle his emails, and she responds to different individuals according to defined protocols and processes. However, if that executive is not informed about what the content of his emails were, he could find himself in a decision-making meeting, unaware of the contents of a critical email. Therefore, a need arises to maintain awareness and oversight, without giving up the efficiencies that come from delegating various tasks.

Therefore, it is important to have processes in place that focus on creating checks and balances to keep you informed about what is going on, while at the same time, maintaining the efficiency needed to keep your business on a pathway to growth. This will allow you to delegate the right tasks to the right people.

Understand what the capabilities are of your team, and then delegate based on the individual skill sets. It can be tempting to not trust the team enough to delegate tasks, thus allowing you the need to oversee everything. I advise leaders that if you don't trust your team enough to delegate, then you have the wrong team. It is just that simple.

People, with the right skill sets, and who have proven you can rely on them, need to feel that you trust them. Otherwise, you simply will not get their very best effort and in the long run, this will have a negative impact on your business and its ability to grow. If you must oversee every aspect of your business, then you can't focus on taking your business forward. Delegation is the key to allow you time to concentrate on the larger goals of your business, while still moving forward with your strategic plan.

Delegation, therefore, is a fine balancing act. Think of your team as an engine. If given too much fuel, the engine will flood and stall out; too little fuel, the engine won't be able to run at all. Your oversight needs to be balanced to allow your engine to run at its optimal level, without being flooded or starved of its necessary fuel.

Look at the ROI of your business. If the owner is drawing a salary of $100,000 a year but getting actively involved in clerical work versus more of a leadership role, then is this really a good ROI? Instead, this could be delegated to an administrative individual, whose salary is lower, thus freeing up that owner to work on income generating tasks more appropriate to his position in the business. Don't waste your time doing tasks that would be better off delegated, but instead, keep focused on getting the best return on your investment from your team.

This is a data-driven decision but one that also needs to factor in the skills of your team. Thus, you can build a strong and effective team.

However, you might have a trustworthy team, but you see holes in their skills, making it difficult to delegate various tasks, even though they are tasks that should be delegated. Additionally, you might find that you don't have anyone on your team with the right mix of skills to take on specific tasks, leaving them on your plate and taking away time necessary for other critical aspects of your business. This is where hiring and training become critical.

Hiring & Training

Part of the hiring process is finding the individuals that will complement your team in terms of skills and experience. Let's face it; you can't possibly know how to do everything. You will need to hire others with the skills you lack, to allow you more time to focus on generating income for the business, and to not have to spend the hours learning how to do it yourself.

That doesn't mean that you shouldn't have an idea about how everything is done in your business. As an owner, you still need to have a measure of oversight. But the nitty-gritty details might be better left to a skilled employee versus doing it yourself.

However, when you are choosing to hire someone, it can be easy to focus on the skills they have and to ignore other potential issues. I have found, however, that you also need to determine how well they will fit in and work with your team. You want to be able to trust them, but you need your team to trust them as well. To build a strong team that works as a cohesive unit, you need to be aware of the personality types within your team. Thus, when you hire a new individual, you can take advantage of their skills but also work to have them become a seamless part of your team and its culture.

I also want you to understand that individuals might be a good fit for your company but need additional training to become as proficient in their skills as you need them to be. Don't hesitate to consider these individuals. A good attitude and willingness to learn can be more beneficial than the right skills paired with a bad attitude. You do need individuals with skills, but keep in mind that attitude can't be taught. Most other things can be taught.

Good attitudes can enhance the culture of your business and build an environment that focuses on growth and a willingness to learn. Technical skill sets, however, require you to hire someone who is already proficient or has the right background. Still, you want to make sure that they bring the right attitude to your company. You need to have the right processes in place to identify and hire the right talent for your business as it grows.

As part of your processes, you need to have a path for training those individuals on your team that may need to expand or strengthen their skill sets. This process is key to create consistency in skill sets, and to create a level of depth in your organization. Many small to medium-sized businesses lack the depth at each position needed to handle an emergency or an absence by a specific employee. Cross-training is key to growth, because as your company gets bigger, you have individuals already trained to step in and assist in key areas.

This training can also allow you to find individuals on your team that you can promote to key areas within the business. At times, you don't need to look outside your company, because what you are looking for may already be on your team.

By creating a skill set within your team, you are also contributing to your succession plan. Every position needs to have a contingency or succession plan to address the loss of the current employee. Cross-training can be part of that plan but also allows you to put key people in place in anticipation of retirements, or of employees being promoted within your business or moving on to another company as part of their overall career goals.

You need to be creating the leaders and managers that are being brought up the ladder, so to speak. If you are training people and giving them a path to follow to move up in your business, then you are also building a loyalty that is likely to make them stay with your business and continue to contribute to it. At the same time, you are creating leaders, which means that you can continue to delegate as your business grows and changes.

This means that you are also giving yourself a choice between hiring outside of the business or promoting from within. If you aren't providing training, then you are limiting the possibilities, and forcing yourself to go out into the marketplace on a regular basis to find the skills you need. However, hiring outside of your business can bring fresh ideas, so there needs to be a balance when choosing individuals to fill various positions within your company.

Throughout this chapter, I have talked several times about processes. They are a part of your production and your hiring of key personnel, and are key to training your team for success. Yet, for many businesses, processes can become cumbersome and slow down the progress of your team. How can you be sure that your processes are effective and continue to be efficient?

Streamlined Processes

The efficiency of your operations is going to be determined by how efficient your processes are. For example, McDonald's was a pioneer in perfecting the process of making a burger. It was all driven by how the process was set up. Today, multiple businesses follow a similar process.

Setting up processes is all about finding the best way to get things done quickly, with the least amount of waste, either of time or resources. All of that can be fixed by streamlining your processes.

When you first sit down to design your processes, you need to be thinking in terms of efficiency. Are there areas where you can build that efficiency into place? Doing it in the early stages is more effective than attempting to build that efficiency in after the processes have already taken effect or have been put into place.

Danny Singh, who oversees operations at Marco's Pizza, emphasized processes as part of the growth of this business. Even during peak times, these processes needed to be in place to achieve the best result for the customer and the business.

I visited a few different stores with him, and it was clear that processes make the difference. Even in the back of the store, those processes were critical to keeping up with the demands of the busiest times of the day. One store was a mess, but when you talked to the store owner, his focus was on caring for the customers, not worrying about the mess. Yet that same mess eventually impeded on his ability to care for his customers, as team members struggled to find supplies or were dealing with leftover trash that hadn't been cared for. Additionally, the customers could see the mess that was being created. There was a different mindset, and it was a less productive and effective operation as a result.

In another store, however, these processes for maintaining standards, even during busy times, resulted in a quicker delivery to the customer, as well as a better impression on the customers overall.

The point of processes is to make sure that the product or service is delivered with the same consistency, repeatedly, in the most efficient manner. When processes are followed, productivity is increased, and complaints tend to go down. Processes can help to keep customers satisfied, and your employees are more efficient as well.

However, the implementation of these processes needs to start at the management level. You set the standard, which includes making sure that all your processes are being implemented properly. This means including checks and balances as part of the design of your processes. Doing so will allow you to tweak processes as necessary, based on feedback from clients and your employees.

As your business grows, processes will become obsolete. You need to build your processes around the idea of continuous improvement. When you implement new technology, for example, you need to be sure that your processes are adjusted to meet these changes effectively. Those processes that are no longer needed should be eliminated, and the new process clearly communicated to the affected staff.

Growth means that what happened yesterday isn't necessarily going to happen today. You can't shut your eyes to change. Your processes need to reflect the reality of change, and it is important that you have already designed processes to help you effectively implement changes as they become necessary.

Continuous Improvement Culture

Throughout the building of your processes, you need to recognize that growth comes with constant improvement. As you build your business, you need to build a culture that rewards your employees and team for finding ways to do it better, faster, and more cost effectively, without sacrificing quality. In fact, according to Paul Kalia, CEO of E. Hofmann Plastics, you have to treat quality like a product, rather than a process. What he means is that constant improvement ensures that you deliver quality as a product, for whatever service or product you are providing your clientele.

The point of continuous improvement is to not just focus on what you did right, but also on finding ways to correct the areas that didn't run as smoothly. Companies find it helpful to debrief their staff after the completion of a project, to understand what went well, what could have been better, and what may have just failed completely. This information is key to adjusting processes, thus streamlining them even further and eliminating any waste.

The Kaizen approach from Japan is about constantly looking for ways to do it better. It is about improving waste by looking at your processes, as well as reducing the error rate. Modifications are key to correcting these errors and eliminating waste. Small improvements, over time, can result in big changes to your processes that support growth in your business.

As part of your continuous improvement, it is important to have a process in place to implement the changes and suggestions on how to do it better, as they come in from each of your employees. You also need to be able to set up criteria to evaluate those changes, determining if they will be effective for your business, based on that criteria. Not every suggestion will lead to improvement, but it is important to create a culture where employees feel comfortable giving those suggestions, and sharing how the processes of other departments impacted their own.

If you are keeping on top of the game all the time, then you won't be the business that lingers behind the rest of your industry because you didn't make improvements and adjustments a part of your company culture. You will, instead, be setting the pace for the rest of your competitors to follow.

Culture doesn't just impact your ability to make changes in procedures and processes; it is a critical part of building your team and growing your business.

Team Building

Strong teams can rule the world. If you don't have a strong team that works together, your business will go down the drain. Part of the effort to create a strong team is through team building exercises. These are times where the team can get to know each other's strengths and weaknesses better, recognizing how they impact the efforts of the team as a whole.

Think of it in terms of any sport, especially American football. The quarterback calls the play and moves the ball. Members of his team are meant to protect him, while others provide support in various positions. If everyone didn't do their job, then the team would be unable to score. Your team needs to function together in such a way that your business can score or grow.

It is also important to note that not every business has the resources to hire a dedicated team member for each job within the company. Overlap will frequently occur, as team members serve in different roles, depending on the process and the department in question. It is important to recognize their efforts and let them know how key those efforts are to the success of the company. When your team feels connected to your company and understands they can have an impact, your business will benefit.

Your team needs to be able to work together effectively, and your managers need to encourage a culture that allows your team to function effectively. There will always be personality differences, but your managers can lead by example and guide the team to overcoming those differences, or at least to learn how to work around them.

Part of building a successful team is making sure they are a satisfied team. When an employee is satisfied with their job and feels appreciated, then the team will function better, and your business will grow as a result.

Now that you have a quality team in place, it is important to discuss how to generate revenue effectively. After all, if your business isn't generating revenue, then it isn't going to survive, let alone grow. In the next chapter, I am going to focus on how to generate revenue through marketing and branding.

CHAPTER 4

Generating Revenue: Branding, Marketing & Selling

As a business, revenue is key to growth. The reality is that if you aren't making money, then you will not be able to fund the growth of your business and invest in building your market. The question is how to successfully grow your revenue to fuel the long-term strategies of your business. However, for what you need to fund, it is important to lay out the business plan and strategy of your company, both short and long-term.

Business Plan

This is a formal document put together by a business to reflect your strategy, vision, and mission. It is a way to encapsulate what you want your business to be, based on what you are going to do and your plans for growth. This means it will include key financial information, which can serve as markers to understand where your business is in terms of revenue generation.

As I discussed in strategic planning, the business plan will include a roadmap of where you want to take your business, both in terms of immediate needs and then where your business is headed in the future. You need to understand that these formal documents can always be adjusted, but they will be key to any type of formal growth of your business.

This is a useful document, whether you are talking to your banker to get a business loan or talking with a potential investor. If you are talking to your management team, your business plan will serve as the guideline for decision-making, giving them the platform to understand where the business is headed in one year, five years, or more.

The business plan communicates the past, present, and future of your business, essentially describing what you want your business to be when it grows up.

What makes a business plan solid? This key tool for your management team needs to be logical and organized, showing the flow of how the company is going to grow, and what is going to occur at different stages to reach a specific level of success.

You also need your business plan to be clear about who your customers are, what area of the market you are targeting, what your pricing strategy is going to be, who your competition is, and your competitive advantage, and so on. This is now going to be a formal document, based on the work you did in strategizing for the future of your business.

The other thing that makes a business plan solid is that it sets the guidelines for your business. These include the profitability, what the cash flow is going to look like, what the break-even point is, and return on investment (ROI). These are all the assumptions of your business, based on the data you have. There is naturally going to be some speculation; however, your historical data can give you an idea of where your numbers are likely to be and where you might be able to improve those numbers—essentially where you can grow your business.

This is where your business needs to define your assumptions, create a budget, and determine the financial outlook of the business going forward. Having all this financial information in one place is key to getting any type of financing, either to fund an expansion or to make a capital investment in equipment.

Your assumptions are the logical guesses that you are making, based on market and industry data, which can complement the data that you have on your own business. If you are already in business, it makes it easier, because you are now forecasting off numbers that you already have. New start-ups will have more assumptions, which can be replaced with your own business data over time. You can also invest in getting this data from data management companies within your industry.

These assumptions should also include the impact of government regulations, and it will help you to define your business trajectory, including what your potential cash flow will be, what you will have to sell, and the overhead costs you will have, to achieve that level of cash flow. You can work with various financial advisors and accountants to complete these parts of your business plan, with these assumptions in them.

Additionally, as part of the analysis of your cash flow, you are going to need to have a balance sheet, income statement, and other key analyses. Ratio analysis will help you to look at your business's balance sheet under a microscope, allowing you to identify areas that need to be addressed within the business. This is a key part of the business plan, which is focused primarily on how healthy your business is financially.

For a start-up company, it is important to make sure that you get your business plan right. It will be key to funding the next few stages of your business as it grows and expands.

Banks want to know how your business stands financially. They aren't looking for numbers on a napkin, based on what you think your business might be able to bring, in terms of cash flow and long-term viability. Banks and financial institutions are also gauging the risk involved in your business. The higher the risk, the likelihood that your interest rate will reflect the risk level. However, as your business does well, you will see banks willing to lend at more favorable rates.

This document will allow banks to determine what amount of financing you need, as well as the type of equity you may have to use as collateral against any loans you might have with their institution.

This business plan is also important if you are pitching investors. With most investors, there is a level of risk they are willing to take on, but they need to understand your business model and how it is operating. They want to see your numbers and if you are a financially viable operation, as well as what their potential ROI could be.

Now, this doesn't mean, if your business is fairly new, that no investor is going to touch it, but anticipate that they are going to want a higher ROI for their investment as a result. The better your business plan, and your understanding of how it portrays your business, is critical to successfully attracting investment funding and capital.

Your business plan needs to become a living document, one that you are continually updating with new data. Essentially, you need to be able to test your assumptions to determine if adjustments need to be made. While you won't be making strategic changes, you may need to make tactical changes based on your budget and whether your assumptions are proving to be solid or not.

While you do formalize it, recognize that you will also constantly be adjusting it to reflect goals achieved as part of your strategic plan and the changes to your long-term strategy, which will also impact your business plan. You are going to use it to create the parameters that will define the success of your business. This process will include determining at what point you will need outside funding or investment.

For companies that are looking to be traded publicly, it is important to have mapped out when you will have your IPO, and how many shares of your company you will be selling. Investors need to know how the cash flow will materialize, and then they might accept or reject your proposal based on that information.

From a hiring or HR perspective, you need to be able to plan for the times of growth and the additional employees that you will be hiring to address the increased demand on your business. Then there are the other different departments. The business plan gives them the ability to know where the business is heading, and allows them to make plans for their own departments in terms of budget and priorities.

The point is that everyone in the business knows what is going to happen, and when. While there are always tweaks that can be made, your departments will be able to see the workflow, which allows them to prepare in advance.

Additionally, you can use the business plan to address salaries and other budgetary issues that can impact your bottom line. Major purchases also need to be defined and addressed within the plan. Any other critical pieces of your business will be included.

As an owner and entrepreneur, you need to know your goals and what you want to achieve, and make sure that your business goals are in line with your personal goals. As part of that alignment, you need to define the marketing plan for your business to achieve maximum growth. What is it, and how can you create one?

Strategic Marketing Plan

This is a critical part of defining your business and understanding your market. I am surprised at how many businesses I work with that don't have any kind of marketing plan in place. They seem to just go with the flow and create marketing campaigns on the fly. The result is that they are marketing their business but without any sense of direction. Thus, they weren't necessarily getting the results that they wanted. It was truly hit or miss, with no strategic alignment in place at all.

Having proper strategic marketing involves looking at your business plan and building a marketing plan around the milestones and direction of your strategic plan. You need to be aware of the milestones and goals that are already in place for the business, to understand how they will impact your marketing strategy.

A strategic marketing plan is when you create a marketing plan that compliments your business plan. Some companies try to build a marketing plan without having a business plan. The lack of a business plan makes it hard to define milestones and know what kind of sales numbers you need to have in order to be successful. A marketing plan, without a business plan, is simply a hit or miss attempt to direct the marketing of your business.

The marketing plan becomes strategic when it aligns with your business plan and your strategy to achieve the goals and milestones of your business. Your marketing plan needs to compliment your overall strategy for the success and growth of your business.

A marketing plan starts by understanding your customers, what they want, and their needs. You need to be able to communicate that your product or service can meet those needs, through your marketing campaign and the PR for your business. You need to give them what they want, not what you want to sell. After you know what they want, then you can align your sales pitch to promote your products that meet those needs and wants.

The marketing plan needs to help you to do that. Without a strategic marketing plan, you won't know how to communicate the values of your business, and who you are, effectively to your customers. You won't know the market or segment that you are targeting. Without a marketing plan, you won't have done the critical research that will inform your marketing plan regarding the needs of the market segment you are targeting. You need to determine if you are going to be competing based on price, being in a niche market, or by something else altogether.

There is research that goes into what appeals to the customer base you are targeting. If you look at toothpaste for just a moment, you will see a wide variety, targeting different segments of the market. They are even positioned on the shelves to attract their target market. The point is that each brand did their research to address the needs of their target market. They also understood who their competition was and how to differentiate themselves from that competition.

You need to be focused on doing that kind of in depth research as part of your marketing plan and strategy. As you identify the target audience for your product, your research needs to drill down into what they need, and then your marketing campaign needs to focus on how your product helps them. It means really understanding your target customer and not just making assumptions based on the industry data that you might have at hand.

This process includes researching your target demographic, understanding their lifestyle, income, age, and more. You need to understand who you want to target as a customer in order to come up with the right marketing plan to appeal to them.

As a new business, it is important to do your homework and start out with a clearly defined marketing plan. Otherwise, you could be leaving yourself open to rudderless marketing campaigns that do not address the needs of your customers. As a result, you will find yourself not growing as you had hoped, or as defined in your strategic plan for your business. The point is to appeal to that market segment and align your business accordingly.

When you build your marketing plan, it is key to have reports and input from all the working parts of your company. This information should consider not only sales, production, and marketing, but R&D and HR. The point is that you need to build your plan based on how all areas will be impacted, and to make sure that you aren't squeezing one area with unrealistic turnarounds.

Recognize that these areas will have some skin in the game when you launch a new product. They are part of the framework of the business. Therefore, it is key to create a marketing plan that addresses all the moving parts, instead of just focusing on the marketing campaign itself.

The marketing team needs to understand when they need to start pushing the product, engaging third party vendors, and they need to know the lead time between when the product is introduced and when it hits the market. Production needs to understand how much they are going to need of the product, and when it will be needed. Then there are the costs to factor in for production and marketing.

Overall, this creates a brand marketing plan that can be easily communicated to your customers as well. At the same time, you are making your team cohesive, while increasing the communication between various departments. Thus, no one is blindsided, and your customers are served better as a result.

When it comes to determining if a product will be successful on the market, it is often important to talk about whether the marketplace would even be willing to buy into the product. Many companies create a product that they want to sell, without doing their homework to determine if there is a viable market. Often, their sales end up telling them whether such a market exists, but in the meantime, they have spent time and money on a product that isn't going anywhere.

You must define your market by demographics, breaking down your target customers. These customers could be the end customer, or it could be another business. There are various target demographics to consider:

- Income
- Lifestyle
- Age
- Interests
- Niche/Specialty
- Geographic
- Beliefs
- Ethnicity

This list is not exhaustive, but it gives you an idea of how complicated your market is going to be. Additionally, who your competition is, and how easy it is to enter the market, will also determine the type of research that you do for your marketing plan.

All of this is going to help you determine the best marketing strategy, which will then impact your marketing budget. It is very easy for businesses to get carried away in their spending for marketing. As a result, I have seen businesses that were so determined to be on every channel and platform that they quickly blew through their marketing budget for the year, on a single product launch, yet they may not have necessarily achieved the goals of their marketing plan, perhaps not even effectively reaching their target audience. You should consider CAC (customer acquisition cost) and LTV (lifetime value of the customer). The rule of thumb is that the LTV:CAC ratio should be 3:1.

Size Does Matter

For your business to truly grow, you need to be willing to spend your money to get the most bang for your buck. You want to do your research to determine the best avenues to reach your target market, and then tailor your campaign to fit that market. Are you targeting millennials, for example? Then you may not want to invest in as many TV ads, but instead focus more online and on social media. This is just one example, but I am sure that you can think of others.

The point is that data-driven marketing focuses on finding out as much as possible before you make your decisions, and making informed decisions for your business as a result.

The other business and marketing considerations that will come out of your research include the determination of time frames. Research can also help you to define the objectives of your marketing campaign. Depending on the objectives, you will have a better idea of the type of budget you will need to have, and if you will need to raise equity to meet that budget.

As part of your research efforts, you will need to determine the references and data resources that you will use. After all, you might find one or two pieces of information that you can decide from, but they may not be an accurate picture of the market. Therefore, you want to be sure that you have done enough research to make reasonable assumptions based on the data you have.

Keep in mind that there are multiple analytical tools available to you, so you need to make sure you have correlated and analyzed your information and data. But make sure that you have focused research because, otherwise, your analysis can become unwieldy and not effective in telling you what you need to know.

Technology is changing very fast, and your customers' needs and wants are changing very fast. Many customers think our wants are our needs. Let's take Apple, for instance. Within the past ten years, Apple has changed our *want* for a smartphone into a *need*.

Every upgrade or new feature has individuals talking about what their phones can do, and how necessary they are.

This example shows you that data-driven market research cannot be a one-time effort for a product launch and then never done again. Research needs to be done in a dynamic fashion, recognizing that your customers are not standing still but are moving targets. The market is constantly changing and evolving, so you need to recognize that, and have a process to keep their marketing research on a constant basis. It needs to be a constant and ongoing process that impacts the marketing and business plans, as well as informing your strategic plan.

You also need to be aware that lifestyle changes are going to impact the relationship you have with your customers. Therefore, you want to account for that as much as possible during your research. It may be that as individuals move into a different lifestyle, they may not be part of the target customer base for your product. But due to their relationship with your product, you may be able to adapt your product or service to account for their changing needs, and keep that customer.

One of the important factors of your database is the ability to grow it with your customer. You can find ways to periodically get updates about your customers through web surveys or customized emails with products that you think they might be interested in. If they respond, you will be able to update the database to reflect the changes in their lifestyle that can impact their relationship with your business.

No matter how you do your market research, remember that the point is to get to know your customers and make effective changes because of that knowledge.

The Seven Ps of Marketing

In *Marketing Demystified,* by Donna Anselmo, she talks about the seven Ps of marketing, which are key to any successful marketing plan.

- Product
- Place
- Price
- Promotion
- Positioning
- Planning
- People

Overall, these Ps work together to help you create the best marketing plan for your business. At the same time, these points can guide your research. As a result, you can then make data-driven decisions, which are going to assist your business in its growth process.

The seven Ps will provide you a greater understanding of your market base, as well as what you need to do and when you need to do it.

Once you analyze the seven Ps for your marketing plan, then you can confidently make your plan, using data to back it up. Now, let's talk about each of these Ps individually, to understand how they can be key to driving growth in your business.

Product—This is the product or service you want to sell. It is important to define how you are going to develop it. You need to tie back to your market research to understand how you are going to develop your product to effectively reach your market. This process includes managing your R&D to keep your product up to date with the marketplace.

Think about cell phones for a moment. Many of you know or can even name cell phones that were big on the market, but today, they aren't even around, or are on the outer fringe of the marketplace. Just because you have the hottest product, doesn't mean it will stay that way without being developed and finding a path to keep it appealing to your market.

It takes a whole lot of market research to get it right. Here are a few questions that you need to ask yourself, as a business owner, as you do your market research:

- What need or needs is your product going to fulfill for the customer?
- Who is this being designed for?
- What does your target market look like?
- How are you going to reach them?
- Who is going to build it, and how are they going to build it?
- How are you going to reach your target audience?
- Are you going to make it a cost-effective option, or are you going to build demand for a premium product?
- What kind of quality are you going to offer?

When you are designing and planning for the marketing of a product, these factors need to be part of the development of the product for the market. At the same time, you need to recognize that there are government regulations that are going to impact your product, depending on where it will be sold.

There may also be potential cultural issues that can impact your products acceptance into your target marketplace. In India, for example, a fast food chain attempted to enter the market, frying their food in a beef oil. Now, the problem with this is that culturally, India is primarily Hindu. The Hindus view the cow as sacred, which means no one eats beef, traditionally. When the type of oil they were using was revealed to the public, the chain had to be shut down. Their entry was basically killed because they weren't aware of the cultural norms that could negatively impact their product.

Depending on where you will be selling your product, it is important to make sure that you have done your homework about the potential cultural norms that you could encounter as part of bringing your product to market with your target customer base.

Barriers to entry need to be determined and factored into the development and launching your product.

Positioning—This is the process of determining where your product will be in the minds of your target audience in comparison to the competition. Positioning is going to play on the customer's mind as they look at what product to purchase. For example, there is plenty of positioning that goes on every day in the car market. Who are you appealing to, and how are you appealing to them? What emotional trigger are you going to use to help your customers make the decision to choose your product?

Here are some other questions to consider when it comes to the positioning of this product:

- Who is the target audience, and what emotional trigger are you going to tap?

- What fantasy comes to mind when you think of the product?

- What will change in your life by purchasing this product or service?

- Is this going to be a want or a need for the customer?

- What market segment are you involved in?

- How are you going to be different in your customer's eyes?

- How can you create value for the customer?

Price—Determining the price is going to involve knowing what your overhead is going to be and who your target market and target price point is. Pricing is huge, and can have an impact on your brand image and even the positioning of your product on the market.

How much work is going into the R&D, and what other features does your product offer? When you think of Apple, the supposed leader of the cell phone market, R&D is a constant part of their process. Their product is priced accordingly to reflect the R&D that has gone into creating a cell phone that people love, with a variety of features they appreciate.

How much are you willing to spend on your R&D, and are you going to pass those costs onto your customers?

Place—This process is driven by your decision of where you are going to sell your product. As part of this decision, you need to understand how you are going to get your product there, and how much of a lead time you will need to make sure that your product ships timely and arrives to keep customers happy. Think of the last time that you had been promised something, but then the date of the event kept being pushed back. Eventually, your excitement would dim. The same is true of your target customers. If you promise a product delivered within a certain time frame, but you miss that, you are writing on the slate of your relationship with that customer. Unfortunately, the results won't create a positive experience for your customer.

Throughout this particular piece, you need to recognize that before you sell anything, you need to have a logistics plan in place. Your marketing channel will play a part in defining the logistics of moving your product from warehouses to your customers. These factors will play into the placement strategy that is part of your marketing plan.

You will also need to build relationships along your logistics value chain, determining who you are going to be working with, and creating value for both of you, as your product moves to the market.

Promotion—The chance to plan promotion is what your creative marketing individuals bring to the table. This process involves creating a campaign to reach your target audience. This is where all your research and planning come into play. Now you are stepping into the world of advertising, and determining the pieces that you need to engage to be successful.

Many of these promotions can be based on marketing campaigns, trade shows, and more. Depending on the target audience, you need to determine the right media and what will appeal to them. You don't need to bomb your audience, but instead you can be very selective in what types of promotions you use. Thus, you can grab their attention without bombarding them with emails, newsletters, commercials, and internet ads.

One of the keys that I find with the businesses that I work with are trade shows. They provide a way to target hundreds of businesses or potential customers in one place. It can almost be the entire industry or a significant chunk of that industry. Therefore, depending on your product or service, it might be a worthwhile investment to consider attending a trade show. The networking and sales opportunities can be another way to drive growth within your business.

People—It is all about people, at the end of the day. While planning promotions, you want to tell the story of your product to a specific segment of the population. This also involves the people who are going to promote it, and how they are going to successfully tell the story of your business and its products. The appeal of these individuals needs to relate and resonate with your target audience.

- If my company were a person, what would they be like?
- How do you want to relate to your customers?
- How should your people relate to your customers?
- How should they dress and act, based on your target audience?
- How do you make a personal connection with customers and your workforce?

Think about the message you want to send, even during the hiring process. You want to find people who will be a quality reflection of your company and your values, which impacts the experience your customers will have at the end of the day.

Planning—I have talked about planning throughout the chapters of this book. It is the critical piece. However, as critical as it is, it doesn't have to be a daunting task that overwhelms your business. It needs to be a process that you have in place, with responsibilities divided throughout your team. If they are working as a team and communicating, then the planning process should be fairly simple. The question is, how do we accomplish our goals? How will all the stakeholders contribute? It is an important piece of how your team will work together.

While these pieces are all key to your marketing process, it all comes down to the data. During the next section, I am going to focus on how you can make decisions that are data-driven, instead of being led by your heart or your gut.

Data-Driven Marketing

Essentially, data-driven marketing is based around the idea of using data about your customers to build your marketing plan. Even though it sounds as if it is driven by data, there are a couple of critical factors that I need to mention. There is plenty going on behind the scenes. Today, companies can buy data on all aspects of the customer behaviour. Everything that individuals do today is being captured in a database somewhere. From what you click on, to where you shop online, and more.

Google, for example, created a concept of digital glasses, meant to capture what you are looking at as you shop. The data captured can then be packaged and sold to businesses. For companies, this data can be a source of information about their customers, one that they didn't have to spend the time to gather themselves. In some ways, it is like going to a restaurant instead of cooking dinner at home. Not only do you not have to do the hard work of preparing the meal and then cleaning up, you also have a variety of options available to choose from.

When purchasing data from companies that spend their time gathering it, you can specify the information that you want, and the demographic that you are trying to reach. This allows you to get the exact marketing information you need, to determine the best marketing plan to reach that market segment. This is how you can drill down and find the right campaign to focus on a particular segment.

Data-driven marketing is really all about the database and how you use it to match the best campaign and communication style with a segment or market demographic. You use the database to learn about them, and then tailor your message and campaigns accordingly.

These databases contain more than the customers' contact information. It can depend on how you want to slice and dice the database to determine how you want to analysis it. For example, one company was doing analytics on their database information, and they found that those individuals who bought padding to put under their furniture as it sat on the floor were less likely to default on their credit card balance. The company decided to use this information to increase the credit limits on those credit cards, and reduce their credit card default risk. It was a great example of how your analytics can give you information you didn't expect, but which can greatly impact your choices in terms of marketing and message.

Customer behavior is available through these databases, and analytics can help you to understand that behavior to determine the risk these customers might pose, as well as the type of marketing message or loyalty program that you want to offer. There are plenty of strategies available, if you are willing to do the analytics. Everything you do begins and ends with the customer information.

Keep in mind, every website you visit is sending back information on what you look at, browse, and click. This means that your web browsing experience, including through social media, becomes more tailored as a result. As a business, you want to be part of that tailoring experience.

At the same time, you need to make sure that you are buying a database from a trusted source to make sure that the information is as accurate as possible. Another point to keep in mind is that your database analytics can help you to see ways to cater your product offerings, with the needs of your customers at the forefront.

Now that you are comfortable with targeting your customer, based on their specific needs and wants, let's talk about the impact of your brand and how it contributes to the overall message you are sending to your customers.

Branding

Branding is the image in your head and the feeling in your heart.

—Azadeh Yaraghi.

As far as branding is concerned, it is fairly straightforward. It is about maintaining your relationship with your customer, how you attract your customers, and how you make your company recognizable in the marketplace. What message are you communicating, and how are you communicating that message to your customers and the public at large? The point of even the colors you choose, as part of your brand, is to make an emotional connection with your customer, not just a mental one.

That connection needs to be reflected in your advertising. Your brand's image, and how you are communicating that brand image, is part of making an emotional connection with your customer. You then want the customer to respond to that emotional connection by buying your product or recommending your product. This is the essence of branding.

Now, for many businesses, their branding is concentrated on their local geographical area. As a result, their primary branding opportunities will be through their stores and in their local area. If they are targeting a B2B market, then those businesses will be focused on the type of messaging that will appeal to those target businesses, and help to build a relationship with those companies.

No matter if you are dealing with an individual or a business, the point is to build a relationship with them using your brand message. Aspects of your brand will appeal to certain market segments, while other aspects of your brand will appeal to a different demographic. The point is to keep your brand message consistent across all forms of communication, while accenting what is appealing to each market segment.

That being said, each truly great brand has something memorable about it. The icon or logo becomes a visual representation of that company or product. Advertising taglines can also be a verbal representation, but the best way to create a truly memorable representation is by combining the visual with the verbal.

Your branding helps you and your business to stand out in the sea of your industry. Even if your product is essentially the same as all the others within your industry, branding is what makes your product special, and can increase its popularity. If everyone knows a specific brand, it implies that the brand itself is popular, which draws others to the brand. Your branding helps your business go from being an unknown to a known, with your target customers.

The internet has been key to leveling the playing field for small and medium businesses when it comes to branding. Those small to medium businesses were often competing against the budgets and marketing power of larger brands. However, thanks to the internet, even a smaller brand can have a big impact, because social media makes promoting your brand affordable.

Whereas in the past your customers were likely to only be exposed to your local competition, now you have customers being exposed to your business from around the globe. Your competition is more than just the business around the corner, but that also means your customer base has expanded as well. However, you do need to be aware that social media can be turned against your brand very easily.

Social media has given your customers a platform to express

their opinion about your company and your brand, often within minutes of their interaction with your employees or your website. Sites, such as Yelp, have grown around the idea of others wanting to hear about individual experiences with your brand. As a business owner, you are going to talk about the positives of working with your business. For the customer, there is a sense that they can get the *real scoop* from their fellow customers.

Sites that review companies and brands have grown in popularity, as well as become a source of information for your potential customers. I bring this up because, in the past, companies were willing to accept the fact that there may be an unhappy customer from time to time. However, an unhappy customer can now quickly give your brand a negative reputation that can be hard to repair, with just a few clicks on a keyboard. Therefore, it is important to recognize the need to be proactive in managing your brand, especially online. Word of mouth is great, but social media is like word of mouth on steroids. The current culture drives people online to find anything, so it is critical that the company they find is yours!

Building a connection with your customers can involve supporting associated areas. For instance, if you sell musical instruments with a focus on jazz, are you supporting events at local jazz venues? This allows customers, who associate with the jazz scene, and musicians, to become familiar with your products and your brand.

Throughout this section, I have talked about branding, but to create real growth for your business, you need to be active in looking for ways to grow your brand. It is about more than just having a brand; it is about making sure that your brand is being exposed to new customers by means of new opportunities. Don't be quick to turn down a chance to get your brand out into another segment of the market, just because you haven't been there before. These are the opportunities that can facilitate real growth.

Branding isn't unbelievably difficult, but it isn't a walk in the park either. It requires that you have a deep understanding of your market and the type of people who make up your customer base. Using an advisor or coach can help you to take advantage of the latest branding techniques out there. Don't limit the possibilities of your business.

Wowing your customers regularly takes focus, but having someone who is focused on giving your customers a Wow experience every time, is critical. Doing so will build brand insistence, meaning that your customers won't look to any other brand to meet their needs or their wants. Without a strong brand in place, you won't have anything to market. The most important objective of marketing a business is to keep the brand shining, and to be continually buffing it. To keep your brand at the top of your game, it needs to constantly be updated and polished.

After all, branding is what gets you noticed before people are ready to make a purchase, when they are still hunting down information. Great branding can turn satisfied customers into brand advocates, who will in turn sell your brand to others. Brand advocates can even influence a prospective customer before they realize they are in the market to make a purchase.

All this is great, but if your potential customers don't know about you, then your brand won't be effective. This is what leads me to networking and its importance to the growth of your business as part of your marketing strategy.

Networking is the MOM (Mother of Marketing)

From a marketing perspective, networking is another way to market yourself and your business. As I shared in branding, not every interaction is about making a sale but making sure that potential customers know about you and your business. The reason that I say it is the MOM (Mother of Marketing) is because many small businesses have a limited marketing budget.

Based on that limited budget, not every business can afford to do large marketing campaigns or extensive ad purchases in TV, radio, and magazine. Networking is the key because you can target the right events to reach a specific audience for your company.

Social media also provides a platform to network online. There are constantly different events where you can meet with other business owners, and even potential customers, while staying put in your office. These networking opportunities allow you to build personal relationships and rapport with others, which can then lead to opportunities for you to connect with potential customers.

It is essentially peripheral marketing, which is marketing that isn't about selling but about building references. You attend an event, and you meet someone, making a connection with them. Later, they tell ten people about your business. Overtime, your business reputation grows, simply because of your networking efforts. Net Promoter Score (NPS) is the idea of having more promoters out there instead of detractors. If you are a promoter, you are going to be out there actively talking about the products and the company. Usually, people will be promoters, instead of detractors or passive, if they have had a positive experience with you and your business.

Networking allows you to create more promoters, who in turn promote your business to others, free of cost to you. At the same time, other businesses will connect with you and give you the opportunity to promote them. For small businesses, building that rapport and relationships in their local community is huge. The same is true with online groups; it becomes a *scratching the back of other businesses and thus they will scratch yours.*

With a better understanding of how networking can be a part of your marketing plan, it is important to consider other ways to get your message and your brand out to potential customers. The days of traditional advertising campaigns is coming to an end—long live digital marketing!

Digital Marketing

You need to recognize that while digital marketing is an inexpensive option to get your brand out to your prospective customers, the reality is that you can easily slip into the trap of giving them too much in too short a time frame. The mistake that many businesses make in their digital marketing efforts is that they don't listen to their customers and, as a result, their emails end up in the spam folder, or deleted.

As a business owner, it is important to listen to your customers. One of the best ways is to allow your customers to tell you how often they would like to be contacted. Some prefer daily emails about your newest products and promotions. Then there are those who only want to be notified about major events related to your brand, such as promotions close to the holidays or anniversary events. Whatever the case, listening to them will keep your brand in their thoughts, without driving them away with too many emails, or contacting too frequently.

You need to be proactive in asking your customers what information they need from you, and how frequently they want to receive it. Many will give an email, or join your loyalty program, to receive a discount or other benefit, but they might not be interested in receiving any information from your company at all. If you listen to your customers, you can build your digital marketing program to fit the needs and wants of your customers, and make your brand more appealing at the same time because you are meeting their expectations.

Now, let's take that to your blog. If you are blogging constantly and sending it out, even when you don't really have anything important to tell your customers about your brand, you make your blog less relevant to them. Therefore, it is important to blog when you have something to say, but don't just put out blogs to say that you posted something. It doesn't mean that you don't keep to a publishing schedule, but make sure that it fits your brand message.

Feedback from your customers is very important when it comes to digital marketing. It can come directly from the customer through surveys or indirectly through what seems to get the most consistent hits on your website. You need to understand what they want in communication, and how they want to be communicated with. That leads me to the front line of digital marketing: social media!

Social Media Marketing

Social media has exploded in the last decade. Facebook, other major social media sites, and the smartphone have greatly impacted the rise of social media, creating a revolution. If your business isn't on social media, particularly Facebook and other key sites, then your business is being left behind. Not taking advantage of what social media has to offer means that you are missing out on a huge segment of your potential market. Social media has such a reach, and it is a fairly inexpensive way to connect with a global market, not limited by the geographical range of your brick and mortar location. Even if you are strictly an online store, the ability to drive traffic to your website can be influenced by your effective use of social media marketing.

There are multiple options for use with social media. You can target your local area, a specific demographic, or even a specific income category. The point is that social media marketing can be tailored to reach the individuals that fit your profile of being most likely to buy and use your products and services. There is a whole lot of flexibility that you have with social media. Additionally, you can take advantage of the analytics available to make data-driven marketing decisions. Google analytics, for example, is a great source of the type of information that can help you to make smart social media decisions. Remember, the point is to grow your business, and using these tools effectively can help you to reach your market, and to grow that market, at the exact same time.

If you decide to include a blog on your website, remember that the focus of your blog is about your brand. You are interesting individuals in what your brand is, your brand values, and your brand message. Your blog needs to do a couple of things. First, it needs to provide information, thus branding yourself as an authority. Second, you create a following, thus making yourself a leader in your industry.

Your blog doesn't need to necessarily be constantly about your business. You might bring up a hot topic of the day, providing information from the point of view of your industry and its impact. As a leader and authority, your blog needs to convey information in an authoritative manner. However, remember that your blog is a brand exercise, so you don't want to send out a mixed message or post something contrary to the values of your brand.

You can also encourage followers to comment and give their own thoughts. Doing so will help you to widen your audience, not just for your blog, but for your business. It is also an excellent network tool as well.

Posting on social media is also key to drawing an audience for your brand and your business. It is all about how many likes, shares, and comments that you have. For businesses, the point is to create a circle of brand promoters by means of your followers. They like what you post and decide to share it. Now, you are reaching all their friends, and the chain can continue indefinitely. You are building a social network online that allows individuals to find your business and connect with your products and services.

Look at Facebook. It is essentially a website with a large group of followers. As a result, they can demand money for advertising on their website. They aren't selling a product, but they are providing an audience. When you are active on Facebook, you are connecting with that audience, only now they can become the customers that take your growth to the next level.

Understanding the Importance of Your Website and SEO

Your website and Search Engine Optimization (SEO) are very important components of business growth. Yet many businesses I work with don't really understand the importance of effectively using SEO and their website to grow their business. Many don't have a true understanding of what SEO even does. Those same businesses often ignore their website, just putting together a barebones one to say they have a presence on the web.

Here's the problem with neglecting your website. It is a business card, a reflection of your brand, which is at work for your business, 24/7. When you don't provide the information that a customer wants, or make your website easy to navigate, those customers are going somewhere else—likely to your competition. Creating sustainable growth, and increasing your top-line revenue, means that you need to be capturing as many customers as possible through your website.

Thus, it is important that you don't neglect your website. Earlier, I talked about digital marketing having a separate team versus just being part of an overall marketing campaign. Your website needs that same type of attention. While your design and the information provided should align with the overall strategic goals of your company and the strategic marketing plan, you still need to make sure that your website isn't treated as an afterthought.

You should be finding out what your customers are searching for, and constantly updating your website to reflect the information you are collecting about your customers' search patterns online. SEO is known as Search Engine Optimization. That means you make your website search engine friendly, using words that can easily be associated with your product and services. Then, when those keywords are searched, your website is more likely to come up. A word of caution, however. Search engines are constantly updating and changing their programs to adjust for companies that might pad their websites with SEO. Therefore, you want to use it, but don't overdo it. At the same time, working within search engine parameters will help you to show up in searches by your target market segment.

When your customers are on your website, it is important to capture how much time they are on the website, and what they are looking at. It can then be used to optimize your SEO. This information is also key to updating your website, because the more popular aspects may need to be expanded, and other information reduced, or even eliminated from the site if customers aren't using it. Leverage your website to make it work for your business, and help to fuel growth.

Not using the full potential of your website means that you are missing out on opportunities to sell your company and your brand. Today, people don't search their local yellow pages; they are looking online, using their favorite search engine to find the goods and services that they need.

Recently, my air conditioner broke down. I didn't grab a phone book or my local newspaper. I went online and Googled air conditioner repair. I was even able to narrow it down based on my location, so I didn't end up with repair companies that were outside of my local area. Within minutes, I had a viable list of businesses to call. Generally, most customers go with the top two or three names that pop up. Imagine that your company was a local air conditioner repair business, but you weren't online. You are literally missing out on hundreds of potential customers daily. If you are online, but aren't using SEO effectively, you could be at the bottom of the list, not getting noticed.

Most individuals, doing a search online, don't leave the first page of search results. If you are on page 2, then you aren't going to be fueling growth or meeting your strategic goals in a timely fashion.

Selling

When I meet with a new company, as a consultant, I want to know about their sales force. I want to know how effective and engaged they are. At the end of the day, you can spend a fortune on marketing, but if you don't have a good sales team, then you aren't likely to see the major leaps of growth necessary to take your business to the next level of your strategic plan.

A strong, motivated, well-trained sales team is necessary to fuel growth. They are the ones facing your customers and representing your brand, portraying the image of your company. Hire the right people to relate to your customer base but who will also represent your company well.

You need to have a sales team that is hungry for success. As an owner, you might hire certain individuals for the skills they bring to the team, but they need to be hungry to get out and sell your products and services. A hungry and motivated sales team will drive growth, and will complement the marketing efforts you have put into place. The sky's the limit for an effective sales team.

Incentives will also motivate your sales team. You need to have a solid incentive plan in place to keep your team excited, but at the same time, to keep them happy with your organization. Don't be afraid to show your appreciation, because that will drive them to continue to work hard to achieve success for their team and your business. Additionally, you need to treat them well. Be willing to stroke egos from time to time, but it shouldn't get in the way of getting the job done, selling ethically, and representing the values of your company.

Throughout this chapter, I have focused on marketing, branding, and the impact they can have on the growth of your business. However, many new businesses need options to finance these marketing plans to successfully grow their company. The next chapter is all about finding the capital necessary for growth through the right financing!

CHAPTER 5

Financing:
Options to Finance the Growth

The growth of any business is dependent on the ability of the owner to find the capital to facilitate that growth. Most small to medium-size businesses do not have that capital readily available, so the question is how to finance any necessary expansions in terms of production, people, or facilities. Throughout this chapter, I am going to focus on the various stages of growth in your business, and the financing options available.

First, let's talk about what types of capital needs might be necessary, from the moment you start your business, through various stages of growth.

Stages of Business

Depending on what stage your business is at, there are various financing options available. The first stage is your idea stage. This is when you have an idea for a product or service you want to provide to the market. You are passionate about it and can see its potential to be successful. However, you are still thinking through the model, which you haven't tested yet. You are in the stage of creating your business plan and defining the key areas of your business.

During this early stage, you are financing your own idea, perhaps with the help of family and friends. You are essentially trying to give form to your business, but the model of what it will be is still in its very rough, transitional period, which could be referred to as the incubator stage.

Next is the concept stage. This is when the idea has become a model of a business, and now you want to proof the concept out. You are creating a plan for your prototype, showing what it is going to look like and how it will function. Now is the chance to get feedback from people, but recognize, at this point, that you are making a lot of assumptions about how much it is going to cost, how much you can sell it for, and what kind of market is out there.

At this point, you are moving into your validation stage. Selling your first product and getting feedback from your first customer is also giving you initial market feedback, as you learn what the customer liked and didn't like about your product or service. From that point onwards, you are going to be tweaking and customizing your product or service, to level up to mass production or a roll out of the service, to a larger customer base. Depending on the service or product, you need to optimize it for the market segment you are targeting.

This would naturally lead into an expansion phase, which is really one of the first major growth aspects of your business. You are now actually prepping for larger production, and making necessary tweaks to expand your market. Your business could be focused on targeting a specific geographical area, or on expanding into a type of business, such as selling on the wholesale market or selling directly to the consumer.

Based on what your expansion looks like, you will have different challenges that might impact the type of financing options available to your business.

At this point, you have become an established company, and hopefully are still growing and having a positive impact on your industry. True, an established business could still be working to reach profitability, but the focus at this point should be on growth and continually progressing toward the goals of your strategic business plan.

The point is to continue the growth cycle of your business. However, to keep your business growing, you need to be able to access capital to support that growth. Now, let's talk about how you are going to access that capital.

Financing Options

When it comes to financing options, the variety available are directly related to the stage of your business. I have spent time talking about strategic planning, and your financing needs should be part of that plan. Goals need to be funded, so it is important to define the points in your business where you will need infusions of capital to reach that next goal and prepare for them.

I also want to point out that no matter the financial option, you are going to have to be an advocate for your business. The individuals in the position to make decisions will not have the same passion for your business. They are analyzing the numbers, so it is important that you can knowledgeably discuss the financial health of your business, and share your passion as well.

Personal Financing

At the start-up stage, your personal credit is going to be the main source of financing for your business. Even when your business reaches the point of being viable, it may still be too new for a bank or other financing source to consider advancing funds on the business's merit alone.

During the early stages of your business, you might also tap family and friends to invest in your business. It is important to recognize that you want to clearly define the terms of any investment by family or friends. The best agreement clearly outlines the obligations of both parties, and gives you a basis for repaying the investment.

Recognize that in these early stages, most banks are not going to offer you financing, as they don't have a history with you, and you have no equity to offer them as a business. Venture capitalists and other formal investors are also not likely to touch your business, simply because you do not yet have proof of concept, and your business model may not be clearly defined and validated.

Some of the resources you might tap are your own savings or equity available to you on a personal level. Most start-up businesses are going to require from $10,000 to $50,000 in funds at the beginning. Therefore, if you have equity in your home, you may be able to tap that to give your business the necessary funds in its early stages. Keep in mind, the point is to move your business from the initial stages into a viable business that can attract its own funding.

Bank Business Loan

Working with banks can provide a variety of options, in terms of funding, to move your business forward. However, it is important to note that these options are unlikely to be available without credibility. To effectively work with a bank, you need to have a business plan and financials, and be able to show how the funding will be used to further the growth of your business.

Not every bank is going to say yes at your first application, so you need to be prepared to approach a few banking institutions before you get the funding you need. If you do receive a yes at the first or second attempt, then consider contacting a third bank. This will allow you to compare interest rates, and go with the loan that will give you the best overall terms.

When working with a bank or credit union, understand that quality presentations are likely to work in your favor, versus presentations with vague assumptions and unsubstantiated sales numbers. If your presentation doesn't result in a positive answer, then try to find out if there were areas of your presentation that could be improved to give you a better shot at a "yes." Take the feedback seriously, and adjust for your next presentation.

Banks are also looking for collateral. They want to limit their risk, particularly if your business is still relatively new in its operations. If possible, you want to have the business put up the collateral, instead of putting up your personal property, such as your home. Some examples of collateral include inventory or equipment belonging to the business.

Recognize that if your request for funding comes without collateral, the financial institution is unlikely to agree to fund your loan. The other piece is building up your credibility. As you build your sales and customer base, the bank will be more likely to want to do business with you.

Crowdfunding

Online lending is big these days. The technology provides a variety of options, including the ability for people to come together and pool their money to invest in a business or idea. Crowdfunding has been key to many startups, who are looking to get off the ground from an idea to a proven concept.

The pooled money is combined into a fund, which can then be used to invest in small to medium businesses that apply for it online. Most of the online applications take under an hour. Within a few days, or even the same day, you will find out whether you have been approved. This option generally funds from $50,000 to $200,000.

There are different types of crowdfunding. Some are thank-you funds, where they will support the idea, but if you aren't able to pay them back, they are okay with it. For most of these investors, the expectation of return on that money is low. They are essentially investing to support entrepreneurs but not necessarily expecting large returns as a result. The amounts funded are also generally very low.

Product funding is another option, which allows you to fund the manufacturing of an initial run of your product. Investors get one of those initial products in exchange for their financing of the production run.

There is also equity and debt funding, which gives the investors a stake in the future equity of the business, or conditions for the repayment of the debt that occur over time. All of these options are available through various crowdfunding options. In order to determine which one is the right one for your business, you need to know the amount needed, and also be able to identify where your business is in its development.

This type of funding has become quite popular, particularly in the tech world. If you are looking to enter this industry, then it could be a viable option for your business, especially in its early stages.

Incubators

These are interesting because they are funded by individuals or the government. They help businesses who have an idea, or a concept to build on it. They will provide facilities and expertise, as well as seed-funding. It can also be a key way to network with businesses who might be able to support research in that particular industry or field, thus allowing your business to develop its products more effectively.

Incubators essentially allow your business to take advantage of this support to grow and develop. However, it is important to recognize that these incubators are focused on finding viable solutions for their industries. If your product ends up not being effective, that support could end. Therefore, it is important to use your access to these resources effectively. Your idea may not end up being viable for that industry, but you can pick up skills to help you develop other ideas, products, or services.

Angel Investors & Venture Capital—Sharks & Dragons

The difference between these two types of investors is that angel investors are primarily one person, whereas venture capital is generally a fund created by a consortium of investors. Angel investors usually invest in smaller projects, typically up to $1 million. Venture capital can go significantly higher than that amount. Wealthy individuals are pooling their funds to invest in a variety of businesses.

There are often subtle differences in each of these investors. Venture capitalists, for example, are going to be focused on a larger return, and may require a percentage of ownership in order to invest. This means they could also require a voice in the leadership and direction of your business. These funds will often look to invest in up and coming technology, or other areas on the cusp of significant growth. If you are in the tech industry, for example, you are likely to see venture capital funds investing heavily in new businesses that are developing the next wave of apps or other gadgets.

The businesses these funds invest in may not be profitable yet, but there is evidence that they can be profitable in the future due to their fast-paced growth. Venture capital funds will take an equity stake in the company, and then when the shares are higher, they will sell out, collect their return, and move on to the next investment. Often, the funds will sell their shares back to the company, but if it has gone public, then they may choose to sell their shares on the stock market instead.

Angel investors prefer to invest in their own industries, one where they already have significant experience. Doing so, they can provide not only funding, but expertise and knowledge that can help your business to grow to the next level. Angel investors can be a significant source of mentorship and networking, providing you another path to achieve the goals of your strategic business plan. Keep in mind, in exchange for this assistance, you may have to give up a percentage of the business's equity to your angel investor.

Private Equity

When your business has reached the point that it has matured and become established, private equity can be an option for owners who are looking to sell the business and cash out. This means another business could buy out your business, thus serving as the source of private equity. At that point, the buyer would come in and take over the management and day-to-day operations of the business, leaving you, as the owner, free to pursue other options or goals.

Joint ventures allow your business to grow by tapping into the expertise of other individuals to take it to the next level. Business owners may find that they simply may not have the skills or resources needed to facilitate further growth. These joint ventures can allow you to get access to those needs, skills, or resources, while still maintaining your ownership of your business. Joint ventures also may allow your business to grow into a new avenue, thus increasing sales and production.

Mergers and acquisitions are another form of private equity. However, these often mean changes in the ownership of your business. You may have a reduced percentage of ownership, or even lose a majority percentage altogether. Acquiring a firm could be a way to expand your business, or you could merge with another company. Both options could allow your business to expand substantially by giving you access to technology and resources, along with new products or services, which could open other markets to your business.

Venture capitalists often can use their funds to acquire businesses or make changes to their operations, but the intent is generally to grow it to a certain point, with the objective of selling it to make their money. Therefore, you may find these options are more critical to your business if you are looking to move on to your next venture by selling your ownership.

Government Grants & Funding

This is the last funding option that I will be covering. It is important to understand that government funding can involve significant applications processes, and require you to follow very specific guidelines. However, there are often government funds available for specific types of businesses and industries. Various grants may be viable options for your business, but it could require tapping into the expertise of someone who writes grant applications on a regular basis.

There are funds available for sectors or geographical areas that the government wants to grow, particularly technology projects. Your business could benefit from those sectors that have been deemed key for advancement and growth. These are generally determined by the direction of the economy and where it appears to be headed.

Depending on how the economy is behaving, the government funding could be a viable source for taking your company further down its strategic path. You may have to repay some of the funds, or none, depending on the criteria.

Many businesses are not aware of the grants and government funding they could qualify for. It is important to tap resources that can help you to research and find the sources that could apply to your business or industry. It is worth the effort because these could help you to reach strategic goals outlined in your roadmap.

I will be discussing the various options available through the government, in a later chapter, where I focus on doing business with the government. For now, it is important to note how these grants and other forms of funding can help you to take your business to the next level of growth.

However, you might not be sure in which direction to take your business, or how to kick-start meaningful growth. The next chapter focuses on a resource that many businesses don't tap, but which can be key to building a thriving business!

CHAPTER 6

Strategic Business Advisors

Throughout these pages, I have shared key areas that you need to focus on as you create your business to build a foundation for success. However, your particular industry is going to have different aspects that make them unique. In order to address these unique aspects, it is important to find a consultant or mentor to assist you in growing your business and taking it to the next level.

Get a Business Coach or Mentor

If the best golfer needs a coach, then you need one too!

According to Bob Whitfield, there is a path for business advisors. The first stage is when an advisor works with you, and you begin to build a relationship with them. This can happen with a one-off project or a small department within your business. As you work with the advisor, the relationship can grow, eventually allowing them to be a trusted advisor. However, if you are looking to help your business grow and be successful, then you need to consider working with a trained strategic advisor.

Once you have used an advisor as a consultant a few times, you will be able to determine if they are a good fit for your business or not. Use smaller projects as a test of any strategic advisor, before expanding your relationship with them. Once they become a trusted partner, you can move them into a strategic position, one where they will be able to contribute to the strategic initiatives that you have in place.

They need to be really engaged, end-to-end, in whatever aspect they are serving as an advisor. It needs to be more than a transaction position. When it is a transaction position, then they can't give you advice and assist you in strategizing for the long-term growth of your business. In other words, they are only working on one small piece of the business, which doesn't necessarily account for the impact of that area on the business as a whole.

If you are working with someone on a transaction basis, it can be difficult for them to give you strategic advice, because they do not understand your vision for your business. They don't understand what you are trying to achieve overall, because all they are privy to is just one small piece of the puzzle. Without that knowledge, their strategic advice is limited and could not truly address the issues your business is currently facing.

I would also advise you to get a separate coach and mentor. In some instances, you can get both with the same person; but, often, the tools of a coach are very specific to one area or facet of the industry, whereas a mentor can be useful throughout the life of your business as you move from level to level. Their worth is in their overall industry expertise, not necessarily their specific expertise in one area only. Often, they have already been where you are hoping to take your business.

A business coach, on the other hand, can serve as an advisor, holding you accountable to make changes or adjustments, as well as providing encouragement. If the best golfer in the world, Tiger Woods, needs a coach, then you need one as well.

When you are doing something repeatedly, you can pick up bad habits, which a coach can point out to you, and give you suggestions to address them. A coach's job is not to necessarily solve the problem for you but to facilitate the process that will address the problem. They will hold you accountable, support you, encourage you, and guide you. I think that small to middle businesses should invest in a business coach. As an individual, having a coach can help you in multiple areas of your life. For a business, the coach can be focused on a specialty, or give you general coaching.

The nice part of using coaches is that you can drill down onto specific areas for your business. For instance, you might be humming along in fulfilling orders, but you are struggling in the area of marketing. Using a coach that specializes in marketing can help you to move the business into a full-on growth mode.

Think of a sports team. There are coaches for a variety of aspects of the game, from defense to offense, as well as strength training and specific skills training. The point is that each of those coaches contributes to the overall results of the team on game day. If you want your team and business to succeed, then you need to be willing to invest in them to the same degree.

Within the business, you need to have coaches for your team. The managers of your teams need to be the coaches, providing guidance for the development and growth of your team. They need to be constantly improving, and the manager needs to be facilitating that process.

As a team leader, I often would find the areas where my team might be lacking, and then coach them to improve. I created the best team because I saw myself as more than someone who helped to manage workflow. I was managing my team to success through coaching. I helped them to find opportunities to improve, and that got noticed by other teams. Individuals from other areas of the company would reach out to me and ask me to mentor them.

As a business owner, you aren't going to reach out and hire a new coach for every member of your workforce. You want that process to happen internally, and you should be proactive in encouraging your managers to coach their teams.

Mentors can provide a much broader sense of direction, and you might find that multiple mentors are needed to help you in a variety of areas within your business. Also, recognize that as your business grows, you may need to have different mentors to address where your business is now.

Now, let's talk about why you need to consider hiring a strategic consultant or advisor for your business, and what they can contribute to your path of growth.

Why Hire a Consultant

I normally advise the businesses I work with that professional advisors are critical to the growth of your business. As a small business owner, you simply do not have all the knowledge, experience, and skills needed to get your organization into the growth mode, especially if you are actively looking to grow, because growth brings additional challenges that will need to be addressed.

Everyone in your organization is busy and wearing multiple hats. It can be hard for them to look up from the tasks at hand to focus on the strategic moves of the business itself. Strategic advisors become critical to have in place because they are not focused on the day-to-day operations of your business but, instead, can look at the bigger picture of how your business operates in terms of industry standards, and how your company could be impacted by larger trends.

That strong relationship with a strategic consultant or advisor can allow you to leverage their expertise, as well as their network, both within your industry and outside of it. Take a moment to think about your own industry. There are multiple people within that industry, some who are leaders, others who are key stakeholders, and still others that have extensive operational experience. What if you knew one person that had access to all those individuals? Wouldn't you want to connect with them to gather key knowledge about all those people within your industry?

Strategic advisors are those individuals with multiple connections, throughout not just your industry but countless others. They can be your access to another level of information, which is key to spurring growth in your company. They can help you to leverage their network, which is the MOM (Mother of Marketing). You can then target some of these companies for the synergies that it presents, for your business and theirs. These partnerships can be a key way to propel growth along your strategic path.

These advisors also bring knowledge and expertise that you as a business owner may know little to nothing about. As a business owner, you might think that you can get something done with just a little bit of research, to save funds. However, that type of thinking could end up costing you much more in the long run. Here's why.

When you first do your research, you do not know what you do not know. Therefore, the process takes longer to complete, and may require more revisions to address your needs as a result. Those multiple revisions are taking manpower away from other areas of your team, creating an internal cost that might not necessarily be apparent in the numbers right away.

Sometimes you end up paying heavy costs because you didn't know about specific regulations or other key information, which could mean penalties and other costs to adjust, or to redo work that has already been completed. It could end up making the entire transaction cost more than it should, which is a blow to your business's bottom line.

For example, one business that worked in imports and exports did not get an export advisor to facilitate the process for them before they started importing and exporting to the United States. They made a small mistake. While they thought it would be easy to work between Canada and the United States—that it should be a no-brainer—that small mistake ended up having big consequences.

They brought a piece of equipment from the United States into Canada to work on it. Yet, due to not having the paperwork filled out correctly, they ended up having to pay duty on that piece of equipment when they returned it to the United States, because it was originally made in China. Working with an advisor would have saved them from having to pay that duty tax, but because they decided to take what seemed to be the less costly route, they ended up not saving on their costs as they had originally planned.

Had they talked to an advisor, they would have understood the paper trail they would need to have in order to transfer that equipment back and forth between the two countries, while acknowledging its original country of origin.

This is just one area that has a complex process, but it can serve as a lesson for all business owners. If you are going to be importing or exporting, then get an advisor to assist you in the process, and help you to understand the technicalities involved in the process, to avoid having your products stranded across the border.

These types of advisors aren't limited to exports and imports. You can hire a management advisor who can focus on areas that your management team can work on, to improve the overall management of your business as you work toward key strategic goals. If you see an advisor isn't bringing value to your business, you can sever the relationship, but this will give you the opportunity to test the waters and potentially jumpstart growth in key areas of your business.

These strategic advisors can be professionals in multiple areas, including lawyers, accountants, insurance brokers, and more. They are experts from industry to industry, and can serve in a variety of functions. Depending on what industry your business is in, you might need some or all of them. It is usually prudent to have the relationships in place sooner rather than later, to help you to grow your business even faster. The ROI on that investment can be huge.

When looking to hire a consultant, you need to look at their qualifications. Depending on what industry you are in, you need to make sure they have some background in your industry or the industry you are looking to explore. How well are they embedded in the industry? What is their specific area of expertise, and how many years have they been practicing in that particular field? If they cross industries, then you want to know what percentage of their business comes from your industry.

This is also the time to get referrals—individuals who have worked with them—to let you know what you can expect from the advisor. For example, if they don't get back to clients in a timely fashion, it might end up breaking the deal.

Do you have confidence in them? If you don't have that confidence, then you are not going to feel comfortable sharing critical pieces of information about your business, which is going to handicap them from successfully completing the necessary strategic tasks that you originally hired them to complete.

I want to stop here and note that no matter how much confidence and trust you have in your advisor, you need to make sure that you have a confidentiality agreement in place before you share any critical pieces of information about your business. This will allow you to protect any proprietary information, and limit what they can share with one of your competitors, if they are working with one of yours within the industry. This agreement will serve as a protection; if they want to write a book, they will not be able to include information about your business without your approval.

Fees are also important. There need to be defined milestones as part of the fee structure, so you can understand exactly what you will be paying for and what you can expect to receive. Do your research to make sure the fees are reasonable and affordable for your business.

This means you might not be able to afford to hire the best in the business, because their fees are outside of your budget. However, that doesn't mean you won't be able to tap into that expertise in the future. Consider a stepping stone advisor that matches your budget, but will still be effective in moving your business in the direction you want it to go!

Consultants can also be a resource regarding research and development (R&D). Using consultants can assist you in vetting new ideas and the best way to move them forward. You want to do something in a different ways, and consultants are often engaged in cutting edge aspects of your industry. They can give you a fresh perspective and help to jumpstart a major change in how you do business or what you offer as part of your business.

Think for a minute about a product that you have recently developed and are looking to bring to market. Perhaps you are trying to reach a different demographic of the market than you have before. Your business could also be looking to expand its offerings, to build a greater market share or to break into a new market altogether. You might also need to make tweaks, or just need someone to come in and tell you that the product isn't going to work.

They can also be a resource when you have a critical problem but are struggling to come up with an effective solution. You might not have the expertise internally, and that is where a consultant comes in. They can be part of your brainstorming process to help you effectively find the best solution for your business.

Consultants can be helpful in diagnosing the problem, and then assist in implementing the solution. Using these experts can really be key to jumpstarting the growth in any aspect of your business.

The point is that using a consultant can help you to shorten the lifecycle of all these different processes, allowing you to get to market faster, and positively impacting your bottom line sooner.

Business Advisors for Working with the Government

Business consultants or advisors can save your business a lot of time and money. They can be a source of information that allows you to avoid costly mistakes as you grow your business. At the same time, they can be helpful in training your staff, so you can hire them to start a process, and then use your own team to finish the process.

Working with the government brings a unique set of challenges; as a result, you may find consultants key to maneuvering through the potential pitfalls and setbacks that can come with attempting government work. Your business can thrive and make significant strides working with the government, but you also must account for the increase in reporting, and some redundancy that comes with government work.

The old joke about everything in triplicate just about says it all. That being said, consultants can help you to manage that process, giving you key markers to assist your staff in meeting government deadlines for reporting and producing.

There are also those inside the government whose job it is to encourage and assist specific types of businesses to apply for government work. For example, the government might be trying to encourage small or minority owned businesses to apply for certain contracts or grants. They will then set up individuals who can be a resource for these types of businesses.

As a consultant, I can help you to find and tap into opportunities that you never considered, which might be available to your business. Growth can happen because you took the time to find out more about the chances available to you and your company. Don't hesitate to use the network of your consultant to mine for those opportunities, because they could be the platform that allows you to take your business to the next level.

Advisors can come in, give you advice, and then leave you to complete the process yourself. Others might stay with you from the beginning to the end of that project, becoming a teaching tool for your team. Others may serve as a resource, but your team does the heavy lifting on their own. You decide the level of engagement that you want from the consultant.

One of the ways that I have used consultants is to bring them in to map out processes. You might be in a state of growth and having two or three individuals doing the same task. Everyone might do it a little differently, but having those processes mapped out can allow you to find the best way for everyone to do it. The consultant might even be able to offer tips about how to complete that task in a different way that no one had done before. The point is to tap into a new perspective to allow your business to thrive and level up for growth. The consultant also brings the industry best practices with them, and can help you redesign your processes to industry standards.

The reality is that you are so involved in your business, you can't always think outside of the box. Consultants and advisors help you to think outside of the box, which is key to the growth of your business. They know what is going on in other businesses, and can help you to find a better and more efficient way to get things done.

Finally, I want to point out that networking is so important, and consultants can be a key to facilitating that. They can provide you access to other businesses, assist you in connecting with the right department to work for the government, and so much more. The network of a quality consultant is broad, and can give you access to opportunities that will just expand the base of your business, as well as jumpstart growth.

Businesses can also tap into counseling services offered by the government, which typically gives your business access to advisors. These advisors can advise them on strategic approaches to get where they want to go, or figure it out, assist them in finding resources within the government, and letting them know about key programs.

They can also be a resource to connect with various government funding and grants. You, as a business owner, might not know about all the options that are available. I highly encourage businesses to consider what might be available to them at a local and federal level. Tap into these resources because, many times, they are free advice that can help you to take your business to the next level!

There are a variety of ministries that provide different resources, and even potential funding. What do you want to do? Take the time to look for a ministry that might be focused on that area. There can also be similar offices or departments at the local level, so be willing to do the work to find these resources, and tap into them locally.

Business Schools

This is a great resource for businesses. The government will often fund these schools to carry out different types of research. As a business, you could get R&D done cost-effectively by allowing them to use your business as part of their research. Now, this might not be available for every industry, but if your business is part of one of the areas of focus, such as innovation in technology, automation in production, or advance manufacturing, then it might be worth your time to partner with them.

Another opportunity is to take advantage of internships or co-op situations that allow you to tap into the student body for potential new employees or interns. Your business benefits from their recent training and, at the same time, those individuals can gain valuable experience they need for their career and, potentially, their own business in the future.

Tapping business schools can be a great way for you to give back to your industry, grooming the leaders that will continue to move it forward. Growth for your business can often be tied to the growth of an industry or a market.

Accelerators & Incubators

These are great resources for businesses looking to grow. These are often funded by a combination of business and government funding. As a resource, accelerators and incubators can provide experience and expertise that you can tap to benefit your business.

They could also offer funding and programs that bring industry experts together in one place, allowing businesses to be able to tap these experts without breaking the budget in terms of consultants or advisors. Use them as sounding boards. They also are helpful in doing R&D research because they can be the space you need to work out an idea, without having to outfit your own facility. They may also be able to help with the testing, if it falls in line with their mandate and funding.

Some of these accelerators or incubators can also give assistance in bringing a product to market. However, keep in mind that these options are typically based on specific industries that they are charged with supporting. Therefore, you might find them to be a better fit for your business if you are involved in the industries receiving the highest focus from the government, and the marketplace as a whole.

If the government helps with the testing, they may decide they want your product, and if they do, then it is as if you already have a first bid. Therefore, if you are focused on a technology industry, you might want to really focus on the opportunities that could be available through these accelerators, especially if they are being funded by the government.

Now that I have shared with you the benefits of consultants and advisors, along with the different options available, let's talk about finding the best way to reach your market.

CHAPTER 7

Ecommerce Versus Brick & Mortar— The Future is Here to Stay

For a business owner, the route to market needs careful navigation. Choose the wrong one, and your product will never be seen by the right potential customers, leaving your business struggling, or even shut down. The question is: Should you go the ecommerce route, or have a traditional brick and mortar location?

At this junction, it must be said that each route has its own pros and cons. For example, the market reach of a brick and mortar location is limited by geography. Additionally, this type of location can produce significant levels of overhead, in terms of hiring employees, renting a space, and then bringing in stock. Plus, you can only be physically open so many hours in a day. Therefore, your selling potential is limited to just a portion of the possible hours in a day, a week, or a month.

Ecommerce, on the other hand, can mean significantly less inventory, minimal overhead in terms of employees and space, plus selling hours that are never-ending, because the internet never turns off. Still, there is something to be said for individuals being able to come in and physically touch a product. While it might be fine to order some items off the internet without looking at them, many others might be an easier sell if an individual can go somewhere to have a tactile experience with the product.

Take a couch, for instance. While it might look beautiful online, you might feel differently seeing it in person. Plus, you want to test it for comfort and be able to envision how much space it will need in your room. This is just one example, but there are many others where your customers want more than a picture on a screen.

However, for those who already have a brick and mortar location, the question could be, is it worth expanding up to ecommerce? You might be very successful with the customer base that you already have, and see expanding onto the internet as a costly endeavor with a limited potential upside. You might have a small web presence to direct individuals to your brick and mortar location, but it isn't the same as actually selling your products online. Let's talk about why this expansion is crucial to the growth of your business!

The Future is Here to Stay

The jury is still out regarding the death of brick and mortar. Regardless of whether brick and mortar locations are going away in the face of ecommerce, it is important to recognize that ecommerce is the future, and it is here to stay. As a society, we aren't going backwards. That genie can't be put back into the bottle.

People are shopping online in increasingly larger numbers. The statistics, over time, have shown that brick and mortar are still making the most sales, but ecommerce is definitely on the rise. The recent data shows that online consumer product sales were 16% of the overall pie. The rest of the 84% sales were in retail stores. However, a whole lot of the retail store sales were driven by the digital presence of those retailers.

If you have a business, most individuals are going to check out your business by using an internet search engine. Those businesses who are not online, thus missing that online presence, are missing out on a huge chunk of potential customers, both those that want to check you out and those that want to buy.

Even if you have a large retail presence, an online presence allows you to tap into those potential customers who want to do their research before coming into the store to make a purchase. These customers may still like to shop in a brick and mortar store, but they want to get an idea of your offerings before they get to your store.

I know, personally, when I was shopping for furniture for my new home, that I went online and looked at multiple furniture stores' websites before I went into the store to make my purchase. I wanted to physically see what I was buying but know in advance what they offered, and their price points made my time in their brick and mortar location more efficient, less overwhelming, and less time-consuming.

I already knew what I liked and what I wanted to look at, and then I was able to check out the quality to determine what I was going to purchase. That being said, there is a whole segment of customers that will only shop online. However, most customers fall into the category of having certain items that they will buy online, and others that they will only buy in a brick and mortar location.

Ecommerce has not reached the position where you can give customers an experience similar to the one they get in a brick and mortar store in terms of being able to experience the product with their five senses. The technology behind ecommerce is continually advancing, so who knows what the future will bring?

Depending on the ROI of your brick and mortar location, a move to ecommerce could be the right step for your business. For start-ups, ecommerce can be an easy way to enter the marketplace, without the same high investment of a brick and mortar location. Depending on your product and services offered, an online store could be a way to ease into the market and allow you to decide if you want to add a brick and mortar component at a later time. If your product or service doesn't make a splash on the market through online sales, it could be one way to judge whether a brick and mortar store could be successful.

Amazon is one example of an online retailer moving into the brick and mortar space. That just tells you that only channel retailers are shifting towards having both methods available to them. The stores might not sell as much inventory, but they provide customers a chance to check out the technology and products before they make the purchase. Many retail brick and mortar stores for larger companies, such as Apple and Microsoft, are based on the idea of making their presence felt in the retail arena.

However, keep in mind that brick and mortar have their limitations. If you aren't a big retailer with multiple locations, the geographical reach of a brick and mortar location could be significantly less than that of an online store. Your brick and mortar location can only target so many customers, based on your market, location, and general foot traffic. Using analytics, you can cater your online marketing to target an audience around the globe.

One of the key advantages of brick and mortar is the tangibility of the experience, while the disadvantage is that the experience is limited to a certain number of people. Online is also the key place to connect with your millennial customers. It is here, and it is going to continue to grow. From a strategy perspective, what is your target audience, and how can you translate into ecommerce? Where is your growth path headed? Do you need to be an only channel, or Omni channel?

Transition from Brick and Mortar to Online Business

Before you decide if you are going to remain brick and mortar, or take your online business to brick and mortar (if at all), it is important to determine what your strategy is going to be in the future.

One business I worked with was 100% brick and mortar. Over the next couple of years, they transitioned to a completely online model, leaving only one flagship brick and mortar store. Their strategy for the business changed and, within a few years, they had executed a complete change in the direction of how they interacted with their customers and their market share.

They shifted their product offerings, and their customer base changed completely. The owners were targeting millennials. Although it hurt them in the short term in their revenue, they saw the long-term results, because their overhead wasn't being hit by carrying all the overhead from these brick and mortar stores.

If you have one or multiple brick and mortar stores, there are a whole lot of costs that simply do not come into play through ecommerce. The money you save can be used to develop your product line through R&D, potentially give a discount to your customers, or even just capitalize to grow your business.

The transition aspect is based on your strategy for your business. You need to know what you want and where you want your business to go. Ecommerce can provide another way to create growth where you might have been experiencing stagnation. Even if your brick and mortar store(s) are doing well, it is important to recognize that you can't be relying only on what you did in the past. You need to constantly be looking for ways to improve and move your business forward.

What are you offering, and what is the nature of your customers? How do they like to shop? You, as a business, need to do a lot of research to understand how you best interact with your customers, and then use that information to determine the best strategy for your business as it moves forward. After all, if your customers primarily connect with you through your brick and mortar location, and your customers are not going to primarily be millennials, then you may want to continue a strategy that supports brick and mortar. However, if you are targeting a different demographic, then you need to be prepared to meet them on the platform they are most comfortable with versus the one that you are most familiar with.

You need to understand that this is meant to be the basis of your long-term strategy. Consider testing the waters by starting your ecommerce business, while maintaining your brick and mortar. You can then manage the transition effectively versus finding yourself moving too quickly and finding that your revenue has dropped so much that you can't grow your ecommerce business at all.

Online Business: An Independent Operation

An online business needs to be run like an independent operation, separate from your retail brick and mortar store. The reason is that an online business has a different target audience, so you need to give it the right attention, instead of just setting up a website and hoping your customers will visit your site.

To grow your online business effectively, it needs its own teams, from marketing to sales and management. This process is about giving your online business the focus it needs from you to be successful. I have worked with multiple businesses that thought they could just treat their website as an extension of sales, but there is so much more involved.

Ecommerce is focused on a different demographic. You are broadening your customer base because, now, you aren't limited by the geography of your location. Instead, you are focused on connecting with potential customers on a global scale. Let's just take one area of your online business that wouldn't necessarily be an issue in your brick and mortar location. Processing payments online means being able to work with a variety of currency, and having a payment system in place to handle orders from all over the world. In most of your retail locations, the local currency will be all that you have to deal with.

That is just one example, but it also illustrates why your online business needs to be treated as a separate entity, not just another department of your retail stores. Everything, from the way you target to your analytics, is going to be different in your ecommerce business.

Digital Marketing

It is presumed that this is born for online businesses; however, as I mentioned earlier, a whole lot of traffic is directed to retail stores through digital marketing. Digital marketing is even more critical for an online business because your target audience is all online. The brick and mortar stores need to be sure that they do not neglect digital marketing, because it can allow you to target a different audience through the online medium.

Others just want to avoid the rush of brick and mortar during certain times of the year, so it can be key to make sure that you have done your digital marketing to help you capture those who don't necessarily want to come into the traditional retail store.

Please see Chapter 4, where I discuss digital marketing and branding, in more detail.

Selling Online

This type of selling can be difficult at times because you don't have personal interaction with them. In fact, they are likely to come to your site only because they are already interested in your product, or saw an online ad. Therefore, when you are preparing your product to be sold online, you need to make sure that you include the information that someone would ask about the product. Use pictures and graphics that give the customer an accurate idea of the size, color, and overall look of the product.

The point is to try to give them a feeling of connection that a personal one-on-one experience offers.

Additionally, you need the data to understand where your customer is clicking, and how to draw them to your website. Recently, I bought a new home and decided I would like a fire pit for my yard. I did some searching to find a fire pit that I liked, and to research what was available. Now, it seems that every time I get online, I have fire pits pop up in the ads and sponsored content.

Once you have the data to help you know where they are clicking, then you need to begin pushing your product or service toward that customer. Having data about various searches of products or services similar to yours, will help you identify the customers that are already interested in buying your product or service, and allow you to target them effectively through tailored digital marketing.

Social media is another cool place to sell online. Literally, everyone these days seems to be on Facebook, Instagram, and other mediums. Social media allows you to see who your customers are, and to tailor your message to effectively reach them.

At the same time, it is important to recognize that the real estate on the internet is getting crowded. It is also becoming quite expensive to get a piece of that real estate online. Therefore, it isn't as easy as it once was to reach your customers. Additionally, you don't have as much control, because you don't have the level of interaction with your customers as you do in a brick and mortar store, where you can upsell them and control the pace of the sale.

Even though you don't have the same influence, businesses are coming up with creative ideas to help their customers have a more personable experience. One such example is the *"Can I help you?"* windows that pop up when you click on various websites. These are a way for your business to acknowledge your customers when they start looking at your site, and can be a way to help them understand the products or services better, to facilitate a purchase. Not everyone is doing this, but those websites that go the extra mile are providing a different experience for their customers, one that is likely to draw them back. You are thus taking customer service to the next level.

As they are on your website, you can find ways to interact with your customers and, therefore, create a unique sales funnel for your online business.

Identifying the Influencers

In the wake of the millennials, businesses are trying to contact the influencers online, particularly on social media. Once the influencers are identified, there might be a deal made in order to get the influencer to promote my product. That influencer may have thousands of followers and, once they promote my product, now those followers are potentially going to start following me, and become potential customers.

Influencers have created an audience, and now you are tapping into that audience to connect with the customers who want or need your products and services. You can use influencers in several ways. They can talk about your product online, wear it, or be seen using it. This method can drive customers your way.

Another example of this is when you see a product endorsed by a major celebrity or sports figure. If they rave about your product, their audience is likely going to start looking into your product as a potential purchase. The reality is that these celebrities and sports figures are the most obvious influencers. Still, the point of using influencers is about connecting with the audience that they already have.

Think about Tiger Woods. If he endorses a brand, then all of the golfers that follow him, along with his fans, are being gently nudged to buy that product. As a business, you need to identify influencers, and tap them to endorse or recommend your products to their circle. The results will be an increase in growth, as these potential customers become aware of your business.

However, to identify the right influencers for your business, it goes back to doing your research. If you don't take the time to determine who your target market is, your potential secondary markets, and your target demographic as you continue to grow your business, then you won't be able to tap into the right influencers to make it an effective method of growing your business. Your strategy won't be effective without this information.

For instance, if your target market is Gen X, but you are spending your marketing budget to tap into influencers for millennials, then you won't have the same growth numbers as you would if you focused primarily on your target market. It is easy to miss your target audience if you aren't sure who they really are.

Build and Own Your Customer Database

The process is about creating a customer database, because you need to know who your customers are. When you first start out, you might be relying on third party sources to reach out to potential customers. However, as your business grows, and the customers start coming to you, it is important to capture that information in a way that builds your own database.

This database is a way for you to build a relationship with your customers, which will keep them coming back to your business over time. The first step towards building a database is to start by collecting basic contact information, such as an email address. Loyalty programs are a great way to attract customers to complete the information for your database, allowing you to send them coupons or gifts. The database can eventually be tied to what they like or routinely purchase, making it easier to customize their buying experience.

Think about Amazon for a moment. Every time you click or do a search, they are collecting information about what you are interested in. Overtime, they can customize the ads you see and even send you special emails tailored to what you have searched for in the past.

Now, with your own online business, building that database is equally important. It allows you to customize that experience for your customers. As you gather more information, you truly can make it a one of a kind experience, one that will make them want to come back again and again.

It is all about building a relationship that will allow you to get repeat customers, as well as turning those customers into your broadcasters on social media as they talk about your product and share their experiences with others.

Many businesses will ask for your email address, even if you don't purchase anything initially. The point is to get you onto their mailing list and in their database. Is your sales team being trained to ask for those key pieces of information necessary for a customer to be added to your database? Have you created a loyalty program that will allow you to capture more information about your customers to understand their buying habits and how you can maximize them?

Think about it this way. Once you have a database, you can now target these potential customers with emails, newsletters, and special incentives. Keep adding to this database because it will allow you to keep in contact with your customers. They can also share this information with others, thus expanding the reach of your campaign.

Loyalty programs are a motivation for a customer to shop with a particular store or brand, either in store or online. Most major brands have a loyalty program, one way or another, and this is key to building a relationship with your customers.

Now, I want to discuss your database. You have worked hard and built this database, but it has grown to the point that it might be unwieldy and difficult to manage effectively. Consider hiring a CSR, who will be focused on managing your database. After all, it is not only going to grow in the number of customers but also in the information you are able to gather about those customers over the course of their relationship with your business. As this database grows, you will need to add database management tools and specialized analytics to manage and visualize it.

The larger your database is, the more effective it can be for all the departments within your business. You will be able to tap that information for customer service and sales, and even for services after the sale is made. You will be able to make better marketing and sales choices to appeal to that customer, especially as the relationship grows.

Customers will often relate to brand, and continue to do business with that brand, even when another company comes along offering a similar product or service. This is in part to the relationship they have built with the brand. Once you have that relationship, it is key to keeping that customer happy and coming back.

Now that you understand what it takes to run an online business, and how your strategy is key to making the transition to an online retail platform a reality, let's talk about one of the most important components that makes any business successful, and that is your relationship with the customer and their experience!

CHAPTER 8

Customer Experience—
The Era of the Customer

The world of retail has always revolved around the customer to a degree. When customers had few retail options available, they were forced to take what they could get. Now, your business isn't just competing with the local businesses down the road; you are competing with businesses around the world.

Your customers could take their business elsewhere and possibly receive the product or service at a cheaper rate. How can you keep them coming back to your business as part of your growth strategy? The answer is, the customer experience!

Customer Excellence

In past decades, companies would refer to periods of time as an *era*. There have been eras of technology, eras of production, and more. Now, this is the *era of the customer*. Everything revolves around the customer, including their experience, and creating excellence for the customer every single time.

How do you stay focused on the customer? You can have a

product or a service, but without having any customers, that product or service is essentially going to be of no use to the business. How do you make sure that you survive, as a business, in the era of the customer? Even when the customer is wrong, they are right!

How do you create that culture in your organization, one where the customer is at the center of all your interactions?

I call it creating customer excellence, not a customer experience. You, as an organization, need to ensure, right from the CEO to the front-line employee, that everyone is thinking and focused on customer excellence. The interesting part is that customer excellence is about providing an amazing customer experience. It isn't about customer SERVICE, but the WOW factor in customer EXPERIENCE!

Differentiate with Customer Experience

I feel that many companies today are focused on customer service but ignore customer excellence. What it means is that each interaction with the customer needs to be excellent. The front-line employee is the one that takes the brunt of this initiative. They are often recorded, monitored, and have the corporate parts of the company looking over their shoulder every time they talk with or interact with a customer. These are the same employees that are expected to create that amazing experience for the customer, with every interaction because, for many customers, that front-line employee is the face of the company or organization. A majority of these frontline employees make close to minimum wage. Therefore, the entire customer experience is based on the interactions by the company's minimum wage workers.

Personally, it seems that is a lot to put on the shoulders of a front-line employee, while the organization appears to take a backseat to the process. Instead, the organization needs to be focused on customer experience at every single step of their process. As a business owner, you need to understand how each step of your business process is going to positively or negatively impact the customer experience.

This understanding of your process is going to help you understand the customer's perspective of your way of doing things, and how it can be frustrating or helpful. While you might first look at the front-line, don't start there!

Internal processes need to make it clear that every employee is part of creating a great customer experience. Here's an example of how this works. It starts with the CEO or owner. They need to clearly communicate their vision for the company, from the top down. Their message needs to be that we are going to do what it takes to make it right for the customer. Whatever the customer wants, then we are going to provide it.

There is so much competition out there, and you are putting so much money into marketing, R&D, and sales, among other things. It takes a lot of effort to get that customer. When they are finally in the door, so to speak, then you need to provide an excellent customer experience, one that will draw them back to your company, time and time again. Through every process of your company, you are contributing to that customer experience.

Let's take an IT employee, for example. As an IT employee, you have developed an application for internal use, which will allow a front-line employee to fulfill a customer's request. However, if they don't understand the customer's needs, and they have the mindset of how to make the application work faster and more efficiently to allow the front-line employee to serve the customer effectively, then the application will not contribute to a positive customer experience.

Customer relation management (CRM) is the tool that brings

all the pieces together. As my example showed, this is the tool that is going to see the bigger picture of how each part and process is contributing to the whole customer experience, and whether it is excellent or not. CRM enables you, no matter what department you are in, to manage customer's requests within one interaction. Essentially, you avoid having a customer bouncing around from department to department, which can negatively impact the customer experience.

Think for a minute about the last time you called a larger company for support with a product after the purchase. Was it a simple process, one where the initial interaction allowed you to have your problem addressed? For many of us, that answer is likely to be no. As companies grow, it seems that the customer experience gets lost.

How will your company be impacted by growth? By looking at every process from a customer experience point of view while your company is still positioning itself for growth, you can create a company culture that makes that customer experience key, even as your company expands and your payroll increases. That is how you will differentiate yourself from the competition.

Now, imagine that the IT employee doesn't understand the process in terms of the customer experience, and the application makes the process more difficult, resulting in the customer being bounced around or not receiving information on a timely basis. Now, the customer's satisfaction level has gone down. They might have gotten what they needed, but the experience was not a positive one, and you may even have a dissatisfied customer. As the time increases to take care of their needs, the more that dissatisfaction will grow. Now you can understand the importance of having an integrated approach, instead of having individuals in silos, unaware of how they are impacting other areas of the company.

When I have talked to IT folks in various companies about the customer experience, they have often asked me what that has to do with them. The customer service mentality has them believing that since they don't actually talk with the customer or interact with them, that they don't have anything to do with the customer experience! It is up to managers and business owners to help the backend people understand how they impact the customer experience.

If they have that line of sight, then they will work in the background to create the best customer experience, providing the support your front-line employees need to create a great customer experience when they are dealing directly with the customers. It is critical to understand that customer experiences build customer loyalty, because return customers are going to be pivotal to your growth. People want convenience and to be able to do things faster. Are you on that trend, or is your business still stuck in providing customer service, without thinking about how to make it faster and better?

However, to understand what will give the customer that quality experience, it is important to know what the customer wants. To find that out, you need to be listening to the customer's voice, as I will explore next.

Voice of the Customer (VOC)

Customer feedback is key to understanding what areas of the customer experience can be improved. Not all the feedback is going to be about how they love your company, products, and services. Some of it is going to be critical of your processes. Yet, without that feedback, you can't make changes that improve the overall experience.

In order to get that feedback from your customer, you need to make sure that you make it easy for your customers to give feedback.

As a smaller company, it might mean investing in a survey company program, using a third-party provider. Other options can also come into play, making it a simple process to capture the feedback from a customer. Keep in mind, if it is a long survey, they aren't going to do it. If they didn't have a great experience, be willing to follow up and find out more detail. The important thing is to make sure that capturing feedback is part of your customer experience strategy. Look at it as an investment in your customers. If you enhance their experience, then they will become walking advertisements for you, and that is going to contribute to your growth!

Do you need to have a customer experience strategy as part of the overall strategic plan of your business? The answer is YES! Don't fall into the trap of being customer service oriented instead of customer experience oriented. One of the ways that this happens is when employees focus more on completing a process than the customer experience itself. Don't be limited by your processes. Be willing to challenge your processes, so you don't get in the way of your company's growth by providing a poor customer experience. Instead, by challenging your processes, you demonstrate for your employees your commitment to providing a great customer experience, both internally and externally.

Too many times, I run into business owners that think a great sales staff is all you need to provide a great customer experience. You don't necessarily need to be worried about actively capturing feedback from your customers. As a result, they are missing out on what that feedback could tell them and ways to improve. Growth can't happen without a willingness to continually improve, and that involves getting feedback from everyone in your organization—especially your customers.

No matter how you capture that voice of the customer, it is important to pay attention to what they have to say. It means really listening, but in order to do so, there needs to be a framework in place to capture that feedback, analyze it, and then put it to use in improving the processes throughout the company. One of the keys to that framework is the CCO.

Chief Customer Officer

I often recommend that companies have a Chief Customer Officer (CCO). It is their primary responsibility to translate the feedback from your customers, and turn it into information that can be used by the various departments to improve the customer experience. Not only that, they will be holding the company accountable to the customer experience standard. If a company isn't committed to that standard, then it is unlikely that your company will be able to build customer loyalty and retention.

However, if you do have a strategy focused on the customer experience, then this should have a CCO, who makes sure that every process and every employee is focused on the customer experience. They are also going to be actively involved in translating the feedback, not only from the customers but internally as well. Don't discount your employees' feedback, which could be key to improving a process or procedure that positively impacts the customer experience.

I always tell people in a business that you have more than one customer. You have your internal customers, as well as your external ones. Those departments that depend on your IT, for example, are the IT department's internal customers. If you have a company focus on creating an amazing customer experience, then that needs to be true internally as well. Keeping your employees satisfied will allow them to positively interact with your customers.

As managers, that means making sure your *customers* have the tools, training, and coaching that they need to be successful. Your team and staff are your internal customers. They need a great customer experience as well, because that will translate into how they deal with fellow employees and your customers. It is a loop, where everyone in the organization is connected. Thus, everyone needs to be contributing to a customer experience culture within the organization, not just the CCO.

Part of the reason I have focused so much on the customer experience is because that experience is critical to building customer loyalty. Let's talk about the impact of loyalty on your company and its growth.

Customer Loyalty

Customers have choices, and you want them to choose you! Building loyalty is more than your loyalty program. It is the experience that your customers have, time and time again.

Many businesses today are using exit surveys to gauge the customer experience. One of the key questions asked is if the individual would recommend the product or service to their family and friends. If they answer above an 8, then they are telling you that the experience was a quality one. If they are answering at a 7 or below, then your company has some work to do to create that amazing experience that will wow them and get them to recommend your company to others.

Not every business has a loyalty program, but many have a great customer experience. Building customer loyalty has little to do with your loyalty program. If your business just puts a loyalty program in place and thinks that is enough, then you are missing the bigger picture. Empower your employees to make it right. Yes, processes and quality control are important, but by empowering your employees, you can guarantee that your customer experience is focused on making it right for the customer.

If you have built your company around the customer experience, then you aren't going to need to have an added layer of quality control. I recommend that you have quality built into your processes and procedures at the design stage. By doing this, you can reduce the cost of quality, and make customer experience part of your organization's DNA.

Always be looking at your processes critically, to make sure that they are in line with the evolution of your business. If they aren't kept up to date, then they are going to limit your employees' ability to service your customers.

That challenging of the processes can't be left to one person. Start by creating a culture of constant improvement. Get everyone on board and excited about implementing changes and making suggestions. Small changes, over time, can create long-term results, as well as positively impacting your company culture. It needs to be something that every employee is empowered to do, so that the company can be successful.

At the same time, employees need to feel empowered to implement process changes. When you allow that empowerment to take place, then you can constantly improve the processes that impact your customers. Thus, you can impact your customers' loyalty to your company and your brand.

Growth is going to happen by turning your customers from loyal returning customers into brand promoters. Remember, if they are responding with an 8 or higher, then they are likely going to be a promoter. However, if their response is below an 8, then you are looking at a dissatisfied customer, or worse, a potential detractor.

It takes three times the investment to gain a new customer than it does to retain a customer. Why would you not work on retaining the customers that you already have? Doing so will help your ROI. While you are always going to try to get new customers, having that great customer experience that retains the ones you already have will keep your business moving forward.

Recognize that every customer experience is going to create an emotional connection with the customer. You want it to be a positive emotional experience because that will make them more likely to recommend you to others, as well as return to do business with your company again. It is about creating that WOW factor for your customer. If not, they may talk about their negative experience, and recommend a competitor. Thus, a negative experience can have multiple consequences for the retention of a customer.

Now, let's think about the customer experience from a branding perspective. When you have a customer experience oriented culture, then that will become part of the brand message. Your company will become associated with that message, and it can be another way to positively impact the emotional connection with your customer.

Clearly, the point is to take your company out of the customer service mindset. Instead, focus on taking it to the next level for the growth and strategic success of your business!

Customization

One of the great ways to provide an amazing customer experience is through customization. Let's talk about this, using an example we can all relate to: ordering pizza. When you look at your options, you might find the pepperoni pizza, but you want to add some other toppings. Sometimes the restaurants won't be willing to add those additional toppings, yet that customization can create a premium experience for the customer, one that they are often times willing to pay for.

Have the option to customize, and that will create a great experience for them. You might find that customization will not greatly increase your costs, so you can do it without up-charging the customer, thus creating that WOW factor.

I was at a restaurant the other day, and it had been about five or six months since my last visit. During my last visit, I had a great dish, but I couldn't remember the name of it. I ended up with the same server and started asking about the dish. I started out by saying, "I don't know if you remember...." The server then proceeded to tell me that she did remember me, including where I had sat during my last visit! Needless to say, she was able to help me identify the dish. That was a WOW factor. Plus, they had customized it for me. I was so impressed that I recognized her by providing positive feedback to her manager, plus recommending the restaurant to all my friends. They made me feel valued, and I know that I will be back.

Your company will be able to reach your customers with that same level of service if you are willing to create unique experiences for them. Throughout this chapter, my goal has been to impress upon you how important it is to create something that sticks with the customer, building a positive emotional experience. When you do so, then you can create a brand promoter for your organization.

However, there are going to be times when you can't give a customer, either internal or external, everything that they want. You might also find yourself in the position of negotiating with those individuals. In the next chapter, I am going to talk about the ways to negotiate, and the importance of strategy in the process.

CHAPTER 9

The Power of Negotiation— Always Be Negotiating

Negotiation is a part of business. While you, as a small business owner, might be negotiating on a subconscious level, the reality is that the best negotiation happens based on conscious and deliberate decision making. Therefore, like anything else, you need to have a strategy on negotiation. Once you are prepared, it can become a very powerful tool for your business.

I love the book, *The Art of Negotiation,* by Michael Wheeler. If you want to get a deeper understanding of negotiation, then his book is one to read. In the meantime, I am going to give you a few key aspects of negotiation to keep in mind when it comes to the growth of your business.

Always Be Negotiating

Throughout your life, you are constantly negotiating, even if you don't realize or call it that. During the day, you are negotiating at work, with your significant other, your kids, and even with businesses for your own reasons. It happens constantly, and has become automatic. Therefore, you need to take it out of the automatic space and bring it back into your conscious realm.

When you let negotiating happen on an automatic level, then you can find yourself dissatisfied with the results. However, when you build a strategy, understanding before you go into a situation what you want to achieve, and if you even want to negotiate, then you have a much better chance of being successful in achieving your goal.

This is a powerful tool for a small business, especially in terms of controlling costs. Depending on who you are negotiating with, and what for, it can result in saving your business thousands of dollars, or even a greater time savings. There are multiple areas where you could be creating savings through negotiation. These include:

- Suppliers
- Customers
- Employees

Here are just a few instances where you are negotiating with individuals from these groups. Employees can be negotiated with at the initial hire, regarding salary. Later, there are negotiations over raises, bonuses, contract terms, schedules, and even potential promotions. Suppliers and customers are both going to be focused on cost. You might want the supplier to come down in cost, but your customers are often going to want the same thing from you. Now you need to recognize the importance of strategy versus just winging it.

Negotiate with Suppliers and Contractors

To be successful in any negotiation, you need to be agile and creative. The reality is that you don't always know exactly what is going to come up in any given situation. Therefore, you need to be able to improvise when necessary, which can be difficult at times. You have to be able to think fast on your feet. Prepare yourself emotionally and mentally. Recognize that each negotiation has a level of importance. Some negotiations with your suppliers and contractors are not going to be as critically important to your business, so you might be more willing to give a little. However, you may be less flexible when the stakes are higher for your business.

What I want you to understand is that for your business to grow, you need to develop your negotiation skills. You need to be able to create strategies and recognize that you are doing business with those who also have their own strategies and agendas. It is not about one party winning or another party losing, but creating a result where both parties walk away as winners.

One example that immediately comes to my mind is the current trade agreement between Canada, Mexico, and the United States. When President Trump was elected, he said that he wanted to tear up NAFTA and renegotiate it. The Canadian government and its negotiation team came into the negotiation with a willing spirit, wanting to create a win-win situation. The impact of those negotiations will be felt by businesses throughout all the countries involved. There are definitely a lot of factors to be considered, but coming into negotiations with a willing spirit and an open mind can help to move both parties toward a successful conclusion.

Some experts think that it has to be a competitive process, one where you come out as the winner at all costs. This is often referred to as the more traditional approach. There is plenty of ego involved when going the more competitive route. It is important to understand that for the success of your business and its growth, you need to be willing to leave your ego at the door.

Make your decisions, during the conversation, based on a strategy. Go into the negotiation knowing what you are willing to give up and what you need to stand firm on. Again, this approach involves a more competitive thought process, so there is definitely going to be some hard ball played, especially from a position of strength.

Know your audience. This is key because you will then be able to gauge better when it is time to push and when it might be better to back down from your position. You need to do your research and then build your strategy around that research. Time and again, I have pointed out the importance of doing your research in a variety of areas of your business. Knowledge is power and will lead you to an informed strategy, one based on an understanding of your business and those you are dealing with.

Going in blind often means that you leave more on the table than you needed to. For instance, you might want to spend a certain amount for raw materials. However, if you haven't done your research, then you won't know what they are going for on the market. You might find that you could negotiate for an even better price because the market is saturated. Yet, without that research, you could end up spending more than you should.

I want you to recognize that your negotiation strategy needs to be focused on getting what you need to make your company successful and to fuel growth. If you aren't doing your research, then you are handicapping your negotiation strategy, while at the same time, hindering the success of your company over the long term.

Part of your research might be the fact that you have a long-term relationship with this particular vendor. What do you know about their negotiation strategy? How can that knowledge help you to reach your goal of a win-win for both parties?

As part of your strategy, you need to have benchmarks set. That first offer that you make will often set the tone for the entire conversation, so you want to make that first offer count.

Another key point is to not disclose your budget. Once your vendor knows your budget, they are going to make sure that their offer uses up the budget that you have set. If you are looking to create savings for your company, you need to keep your budget to yourself. Negotiate based on what you want to spend, but don't be quick to disclose that information.

I know that many of you can relate to the realities of negotiating where you have disclosed your budget, only to end up spending as much, or even more, than you anticipated. Circle around it and see how the conversation goes before you commit to anything.

Another reason not to disclose your budget is that the vendor could sell you a lower quality product at a higher price to meet your budget, but that lower quality product could have a negative impact on your business and your brand. Remember customer excellence, and the importance of creating an amazing experience for customers, with every interaction? Poor quality products aren't going to contribute to your customer excellence and, thus, they can negatively impact your company's growth in the long term.

From a seller's perspective, it is important to consider structuring your offerings in such a way that you can meet various price points for customers. Think of many of your major tech companies. They offer various smartphones, for instance, at various price points. Customers can choose the phone that meets their needs and their budget. Your company can also provide graduated offerings, which can help in your negotiation process.

For example, a bells and whistles option could be sold at a premium, while other offerings might not include as many of the bells and whistles but can still provide a quality product within your customer's budget. That means you can still do business with them. It doesn't have to be an either/or situation, which drives out the low budget customers. You can still make the customer feel good about doing business with you.

It is about understanding what you are willing to compromise on and what you think the other party might be willing to compromise on. The more you know about who you are negotiating with, the greater the likelihood that you will understand the areas where they are willing to bend and where they are not likely to be as willing. Part of that includes knowing what their leverage point is and how you can use that leverage to achieve your aim in the negotiation.

Recognize that both parties are going to have to budge to come to an agreement. The question is, how much are you willing to budge to achieve a win-win?

The more modern approach is truly one of collaboration. If you are looking out for the interests of both parties, it will positively impact your ability to do business with those individuals or companies in the future. You don't want them to walk away from your negotiation feeling ripped off or that they didn't get a fair deal, because that will negatively impact their desire to do business again with your company in the future. Consider it a negative impact on your growth strategy. Win-win situations, however, create a collaborative approach that will positively contribute to the growth of your business.

If you know what your bottom line is, then you will also know when it is time to walk away from the table. Sometimes, despite your best efforts, the deal just isn't going to get done. Be willing to recognize it when it happens, and be willing to get up and walk away. This strategy can leave you open to different opportunities because you aren't willing to take a bad deal just to say you got one. It needs to have a purposeful approach, instead of butting heads throughout the process. No one wants to walk away feeling as if they got the shorter end of the stick.

Doing business in any industry doesn't mean that your business lives in a silo. How you negotiate with one business will build a reputation that impacts your negotiations with others. If they are on your side and feel as if the negotiations were a win-win, then those individuals are going to talk about you favorably to other businesses. It is amazing to me how many opportunities for growth can be opened to your business when you take the time to build a favorable reputation among the businesses and vendors that you work with. Be careful how you deal with these guys.

Always be willing to negotiate with your contractors and suppliers, because it can help you to manage your costs. For example, some businesses are willing to match the lowest offer to get your business. Having quotes can help you to find the best offer for your company in terms of getting products or services at a price that helps your bottom line.

Things are always changing in the business world. To manage your contractor costs, you need to get updated quotes on an annual basis. This process can help you to find a potential vendor at a lower price point. Your current vendor might be willing to come down in order to keep your business. Costs also change, so make sure you get at least two different quotes so that you can negotiate from that. Do a cost analysis from the supply side so that you understand what is involved in the price that they are quoting you. Once you look at the cost analysis, see what you can negotiate on. Perhaps doing a bulk deal can allow you to get a better price based on the volume you are purchasing. Also, if you are willing to lock in with a vendor for a specific period, you might also find it easier to negotiate a better price point because you are locked in to buying from them.

There is a lot that you can do from a negotiation standpoint, instead of just walking in and demanding a deal at a specific price point. Again, I can't stress enough how important it is to make sure that you are negotiating with a win-win in mind.

Negotiate Contracts and Leases

The biggest costs for any business is the cost of the manufacturing of their products, and the cost of their office, warehouse, and storage space. For the manufacturer, their costs are going to be based on how many products you ask them to make, and the quantity, as well as how much it is going to cost them to tool up for production.

For example, a manufacturer who tools up for a small run of a product is going to charge more for that product run than it would for one that will be ongoing in larger quantities, over the length of the contract. When you are working with a manufacturer, it is important to understand that it is likely going to be much easier to negotiate the price down on larger quantities, versus a smaller product run with a complicated tooling process.

How does this impact your growth? If you are able to increase the order and lower your costs, you can leave your price the same for your customers but positively impact your bottom line. Think in terms of your profitability. Also, remember that manufacturers can be loyal if you return the favor. Don't be quick to jump just for a better price. It is important to check their quality before you commit to a long-term contract.

When it comes to your lease, you need to recognize that it is going to be a huge part of your overhead. In order to spur growth in your business, you need to have a handle on all the costs associated with your business. I have seen so many businesses that didn't do a good job when it came time to negotiate the lease for their space. Then, a few years into the lease, as rents are rising, they find themselves struggling to keep their business going. For some businesses, this cost eventually snowballed to the point that they had to close. Small to medium-sized businesses need to be cautious when it comes to negotiating leases, as they can have a long-term impact on the ROI of your business.

Additionally, you must think about the costs of moving, if you decide to break a lease. Changing locations can include letting your customers know where you moved, paying any fees associated with breaking the lease, as well as building out a new location, moving inventory, and limiting the amount of downtime. When a business is down because of a change in location, it isn't making the same level of income, which can negatively impact any growth that may have been achieved to date, and derail a strategic plan.

Another reality of changing locations is that you may also have to reposition your business altogether, reaching out to a completely different clientele. Then there is the cost of bringing product to your new location, if access is less ideal than your original one.

The point is to make sure that you count the cost when negotiating your leases, especially since they lock you in for a significant period of time. As your business grows, your space needs may grow as well. As you negotiate your lease, think about future growth. Is there the ability to lease more space, or will you have to relocate? Your business plan and strategic goals need to come into play when deciding on a location, both for your current needs and your future ones.

Don't rush into these agreements just because a space appears to be perfect for your business. Get a lawyer involved in those negotiations. Make sure you are aware of any potential reimbursements for build-outs of the space. Also, be sure that you understand all the aspects of the lease before you sign on the dotted line. Doing so will help you to position your business for growth!

Negotiate with Distributors

When it comes to the growth of your business, distributors play a key part. If you don't have someone distributing your product, then your customers aren't receiving it, and your business is not making the necessary money needed for its growth.

Let's stop for a moment and talk about your online storefront. Essentially, when you create an online store, you are becoming your own distributor. Therefore, you need to be prepared to consider using a third party. If you do, then it is important to negotiate your contract so that they feel as if they are getting a part of the pie for their efforts.

Distributors are critical to any business, even if you are using brick and mortar locations. When negotiating, remember to keep the win-win mentality. For example, large corporations set margins with their distributors, essentially telling them how much they will make on each unit that they sell. Recently, Apple reduced the margins for distributors in India. The result is that they have a whole group of distributors who are less than excited to carry and sell their products.

When you are negotiating the margins with your distributors, make sure that you don't end up alienating them by keeping your margins high at the expense of keeping theirs razor thin. You don't want your distributors to focus on selling other products at the expense of your own.

They could also decide that they can get a better deal somewhere else, and decide to drop your product altogether. If this happens, it can reduce your distribution network, which can negatively impact your sales.

People pay on value, so if you can show the value of your product, they will be willing to pay what you ask, and charge their customers accordingly. Customers are drawn to their favorite brands, so your distributors know what is selling and what isn't. If your products are taking longer to sell, and then you try to use hardball negotiation tactics, it isn't likely to improve your relationship with your distributor. In fact, they may decide to drop your product line altogether.

Don't Negotiate with One Person: The Customer

When it comes to negotiating with your customers, you want to have a strategy in terms of what you want to achieve, but at the same time, your strategy needs to take into account the fact that you don't want to irritate or tick off your customer. Remember Chapter 8, where I talk about the customer experience? This is one of those times where you need to balance your negotiation on price, with the need to leave the customer with a positive experience, one that will hopefully turn them into a promoter.

The question is, how do you negotiate with a customer, without leaving them feeling as if you are negotiating them up or down, as the case may be? Where does your win-win situation lie?

It comes in the value that you create for your customers. They might want to negotiate, but you need to be sure that they feel as if they are getting value based on what they paid for your product. When dealing with your customers, you want them to leave with a positive emotional connection to your product, with the hopes of turning them into a promoter of your brand and company.

Offering value could be in terms of additional service contracts or premium add-ons that contribute to the performance of your product. Remember, the point is to make your customer feel as if they really got a deal for their money.

Consider offering different packages that allow your customer to decide based on their budget. Layer items to create premium packages, and then charge accordingly. It will make you stand out in the minds of your customers. There are many ways to negotiate with your customers, without making them feel as they are in the middle of a negotiation, thus creating that win-win.

What is the competition up to? You might want to set the prices and not be willing to negotiate, but your customers may want to because they have that experience with your competition. Maybe you don't beat your competition on price, but do you create a premium experience that makes the difference, turning individuals to your product versus the competition. Playing hard ball isn't going to work in this situation, but using a strategic plan can help you to successfully navigate the moves of your competition.

Legal Team

Finally, as part of the negotiation process, it is important to have a strong legal team that not only understands your business but also your industry. It can be easy to find a lawyer that you feel comfortable with for your business, only to find that they are not familiar with your industry, making them a potential liability to your negotiations.

Essentially, you want them to have the skill set to work on contracts, leases, and other legal aspects of your negotiations. You want them to be able to work out the legal language to make sure that you don't end up giving away what you negotiated on a legal technicality.

For example, they might be great with leases but not as good with supplier contracts. You want them to be comfortable with all the different aspects of your business's needs. If you are doing business across the borders, they may not be familiar with international law. Depending, therefore, on the needs of your business, you need to assemble a legal team to address all potential contracts, leases, and aspects of international law. To accomplish this, you might need to work with different attorneys based on their specialties.

Depending on their skill set, it might be beneficial to have them at the table during the negotiation process, particularly as related to your contracts. If they are going to help with negotiations related to international trade agreements, then it is important that they know those trade agreements like the back of their hand. They also need to be able to help you identify any potential trouble spots that you might encounter during your negotiations, and help you to prepare accordingly.

Your legal team is important to negotiations. Your lawyer may be a better negotiator than you, so be willing to lean on their expertise whenever necessary. In the end, it will help you to grow your business successfully by creating win-win situations for you and whoever you are negotiating with, be it a supplier, distributor, or potential landlord.

Finally, you want to keep your negotiations light, and avoid feelings of conflict, which can make things more complicated. Again, doing so will help you to create those win-win situations that are critical to the growth of your business.

The growth of your business is not only determined by how you manage costs through negotiation; you also need to keep up with your industry and the technology. Advances are constantly being made, and if you aren't keeping up, your business could become obsolete. Let's talk about the impact of technology and how to keep your business moving forward without breaking the bank.

CHAPTER 10

Technology & Innovation

No business can thrive without the constant evolution. In the world of technology, the focus is on doing everything faster, better, and smarter. Innovation—essentially thinking outside of the box—can help you to find those connections to use technology effectively, and help move your business forward into a true growth position.

Without the proper tools, your business will fall behind your competition. You might not be considered outdated today, but without implementing a plan to address changing technology, you will find yourself struggling to pay for a major upgrade, or you may be too far behind to catch up.

The question is how to keep your business from getting so focused on the day-to-day operations that you miss the bigger picture, which is evolving to meet the changing needs of your customer and the changing standards of your industry. The first and most important thing you need to integrate into your business is innovation at all levels of your business.

Innovate to Evolve and Stay Ahead

Depending on your industry, innovation can look different. It isn't cookie cutter, as in you do it one way and then you can effectively do that same way over and over again. Throughout this book, I have continued to focus on creating and being a change agent in your own business. Growth doesn't happen by sitting still but requires you to really focus on constantly moving forward.

Whether it is your processes or the customer experience, you need to have your team constantly focused on how to improve, how to adapt, and how to do it better the next time. There should never be a moment when you think to yourself, as a business owner, "That's good enough." When you do, you might as well sell the business, because that attitude will lead to the slow death of your company. As the owner of the business, your job is to continuously find areas of improvement in your business, and task your team to innovate and come up with new and better ways of doing things.

Innovation is critical to this mindset because it requires you to take your business model and look at it from a critical and objective viewpoint. You need to also be willing to take a problem or challenge, and be open to all potential solutions, no matter how far-fetched they might seem initially.

I often tell my clients to eat innovation for breakfast. Innovation doesn't just happen one day when you need it but is part of a larger cultural mindset of your business. You need to constantly foster an environment that encourages you and your team to think outside of the box, to be creative in your solutions to challenges, and to be open to trying something new. What might not appear to be a solution could in fact be the solution that you are looking for to propel your company forward.

I want to stop here for a moment and talk about how innovation compliments a culture of customer excellence. Earlier, I focused on constantly improving, finding ways to do things even better, and turning weaknesses into strengths, while supporting what your team does well. Innovation focuses on finding new ways to adapt your strengths and weaknesses to solve problems and find exciting new ways for your company to grow in the marketplace.

Innovation also plays a part in meeting the needs and wants of your customers. As technology changes, your company can find new uses for it, to more effectively serve your customers. However, it is important to note that an application or new technology, on the surface, might not seem to be a fit for your customers' needs and wants. With a little innovation, that same technology or application could be adapted for a new use, one that no one initially saw coming.

In Southeast Asia, for example, ride-sharing companies are offering more than just rides to work, restaurants, or entertainment. They are offering services, including food delivery, arranging pedicures, and even allowing you to pay bills through their app. Sounds different than the Uber app that you might be using, doesn't it? There was a chance for innovation: a way to address the needs of customers who didn't want to go out into the traffic, and deal with being stuck for hours, just to get food or other items.

These innovations are putting these companies on the forefront of a new move in the industry, to provide more through just one app, and create even more customer loyalty. If you aren't innovating, then your company is falling behind. It is just that simple.

Today's customers are even more demanding, and it can be challenging to stand out from your competition. Innovation allows you to be different because your offering is made in a unique way— one that might be unexpected but prove to be very profitable.

When you are focused on innovation, it gives you an advantage over your competition. That advantage might be in terms of cost, profit margin, technology, or in how your product or service is delivered. The point is that it stands out for the customer, and will bring them back to your company again and again.

Without innovation, you are essentially putting an expiration date on your company, telling the competition that you and your products will eventually be obsolete. Do you want that for your company? Is that the future you outlined in your strategic plan? If not, then you need to be open to innovation and what it has to offer.

How can you encourage innovation? It starts by opening up the lines of communication. For instance, you might think that marketing campaigns should only be rooted in the marketing department. Yet you might find that someone from production or another department has an idea for marketing the product, which your team hadn't thought of before. Do you ignore it just because it didn't come from your *experts?* I encourage you to be willing to listen to what your team members share, regardless of where they are working in your business. Their insights could be the basis for the innovation that you need to keep growing and enriching your business.

These insights don't need to be limited to just marketing; they could be ways to increase production, trim packing and shipping times, as well as implementing measures that could reduce waste. Your team is working with your product day in and day out. Their knowledge and creative ideas could be the basis of your company's next move toward growth. Don't be quick to ignore them just because of a job title.

One of the challenges I have seen frequently is that my clients confuse innovation with invention. The two are not one and the same. In fact, while one can lead to another, the same can't always be said of the reverse.

According to Wikipedia, innovation is defined as *"the application of better solutions that meet new requirements, unarticulated needs, or existing market needs.*" This is accomplished through more effective products, processes or services, technology, and business models that are readily available to the market, government, or society as a whole. It can be something original or a more effective use of a model that society has already created. The point to remember is that your company can be the source of that type of innovation, with a larger impact than just your organization.

In a recent article by Chad Brooks, in *Business News Weekly,* he interviewed entrepreneurs about why innovation is important. One of the individuals he quoted was from Fusion 92's Jacob Bentley, who said, *"While innovation might have slightly different meanings depending on the industry, its core is universal. It embodies the improvement of something that has come before. It is the evolution of convenience, efficiency, and effectiveness."* He noted that the companies that do this well are the ones that will have sustained success.

Brooks also mentioned different types of innovation. Some of the ones that he mentioned include open innovation, disruptive innovation, development innovation, incremental innovation, and breakthrough innovation. Depending on what industry, product, or services, businesses have options available to them. Here is a short description of each of these innovation types:

- Open innovation—When companies use internal and external ideas to advance their operations and expand the market.

- Disruptive innovation—When new products surface at the bottom of the marketplace but eventually move up and displace their competition. (Example: refrigerators and mobile phones)

- Development/Reverse innovation—This is when products and services are initially created for, or tested in, developing nations, and then brought over into developed nations. (Example: Netflix)

- Incremental innovation—When companies make small changes to their products or services over time to maintain their position in the marketplace. It builds upon what already exists. (Example: cars)

- Breakthrough innovation—This is the development of completely new ideas and concepts that don't build off anything that already exists, and is typically a result of R&D. It can be referred to as radical innovation. (Example: the Internet)

While many companies see the need to innovate in order to grow, it is important to note that there is an increasing level of dissatisfaction with the level of innovation throughout the business world. That means, no matter what industry you are in, innovation is likely not the core of every organization. To grow, you need to make it a critical part of yours!

You do not need to be Einstein to innovate. You just need to be open-minded and willing to be creative in your thinking. It involves being eager to not stick with something just because that is the way you have always done it. If that had been the case, computers and much of the technology we rely on today would simply not exist.

Instead, innovation starts with small ideas that you work on, and which grow over time as you adjust and make tweaks. There are failures, but you keep working on it, and you end up with a new solution that could be your breakthrough, or a small improvement in combination with others, which can create significant changes in your business overtime.

The point is to try new things, even if they are just small ones to start. Recognize that not every idea will be met with great success. In fact, you might find that your business has more than a few failures. However, those failures can be used to fuel innovation, and allow for adjustments based on what didn't work, as much as what did work.

When you get feedback from your customers, for example, it can be a chance to look at your processes with fresh eyes. Innovation comes from not making anything off limits to change and adjustments. When I talked about customer feedback, earlier, it isn't just about making the customer experience better. It can be the jumping off point for innovation within your company. If you don't have a process to capture that feedback, then you are missing out on a potential source of ideas that can fuel the innovation within your company.

Do you have someone, and a process, for handling customer complaints, one that allows feedback to loop into the company where change can be implemented? This process is important because it allows you to understand the areas that are negatively impacting your customers and the growth potential of your business. Thus, you can use innovation to fix these areas by calling your employees' attention to the problem, and then using their ideas to address the issues.

Your employees, who regularly interact with your customers, might be able to alert you to potential issues before your customers do. That's why it is important to listen to them, and build a channel for them to communicate their feedback. Then, really give it the weight that it deserves, instead of just dismissing it out of hand. Remember, you are looking for ideas that can create improvement and opportunities for growth.

Innovation for business means trying to do things differently, trying new concepts, and trying to do things in a way that tweaks the current process. This doesn't have to be very expensive, unlike invention, which often requires a lot of R&D and significant outlays of capital. You need to understand that innovation is focused around ideas, so the best sources of those ideas is the team that you already have.

I want you to stop and think about the culture of your business for a moment. When individuals on your team don't feel heard by management or the ownership, they tend to keep their best ideas to themselves. That can really cost your business! You want to foster a mentality in your team that says we don't have to do it one way forever, but we are open to new ideas and ways to make the process flow smoother, faster, or more profitably.

The environment of your company needs to focus on engaging your employees, and helping them to understand that their ideas and input are valuable to the company. Think about it this way. If you have 100 employees, and each of them came up with just one idea—just one—you would now have 100 new ideas. Some might be small and involve tweaking a process, but others could have a far greater initial impact. The point is, if you aren't fostering an environment that keeps your team engaged and sharing, then you are missing out on all the ideas and input they have to offer. Once you have that environment and culture, you don't need to go looking for innovation, because it will be a part of your DNA as an organization.

Now, you might be thinking to yourself, "If I do that, then I am taking my employees away from their jobs and decreasing their productivity." I am here to tell you that you want those ideas. They are worth the temporary dip in productivity because, in the long run, it will mean that your company has changed and adapted, instead of standing still and eventually dying off due to stagnation.

Give them time to implement and try these new ideas. It means that you have to manage your productivity in a way to account for their absence, to work on that new idea, but it can be worth it in the long run in terms of efficiency and overall productivity of your company over the months and years.

Some fundamental ways to encourage employees would be to allow them to access industry webinars or other events. Seeing a trade show or conference, for example, might trigger an idea for them that could benefit your business. There are also grants and funding available from the government to spawn innovation, and to fund R&D. Tapping into these funds could help your company to develop an idea into a viable product or service. These new products or services could provide the next step of growth in your company.

While it might seem daunting to add research or testing of ideas to your budget, there are resources out there to help your company explore these ideas, and support the innovation within your company. Innovation requires having a process in place to capture ideas and feedback, then find ways to test and implement them.

As part of your financial plan, it is important to include a budget for innovation and R&D. These funds are then available for you to tap into when someone on your team comes up with an idea. You don't have to abandon a potential source of growth because of a lack of funding. Over the years, you can budget for innovation, putting that money aside. Along with the grants, other resources are also available to work with your budget. There is no reason to abandon an idea or potential product, but instead, see these ideas as a source of growth in your company.

Another key area is also a hot topic now, in terms of technology and innovation, known as ICT, which stands for innovation and communication technology. It is changing so rapidly, that as a business, it can be hard to keep up. For example, in regard to people answering phones, ICT has changed that, allowing you to provide quality service without having an individual tied to the phones.

Think of this in terms of shift work. If you are open 24 hours a day, you would then need someone answering the phones 24 hours a day. Yet, with the advent of ICT, you now can have the phones answered with a significant cost savings, freeing up employees to handle other tasks. There are so many benefits available, but for companies to grow, they need to take advantage of these opportunities. After all, if you aren't, you can be sure that your competition is!

This is especially true within the realm of technology, which I will explore next.

Technology Adoption and Incubators

When I talk to many businesses today, there seems to be a fear of technology and its capability. Frankly, there are a lot of options out there, and for many business owners, the choices can be overwhelming, at least initially. Still, there is a need to overcome this fear of technology, for the growth and overall wellbeing of your business, and to achieve your strategic plan.

For a business to be successful, you need to make friends with technology. As a business owner, you need to be aware of what technological advances are being made in your industry, and how they can impact your business. Various technologies can be adapted by an industry, and become best practices. If you aren't aware, then you will find yourself struggling to catch up to your competition.

The best way to stay on top of technology is to adapt to it and then adopt it. By making incremental changes, you can adopt new technology without being overwhelmed, both in terms of getting your team up to speed and the capital investment involved. If you don't make those adjustments in increments, what I find, after 10 years, is that your company is now significantly behind the technology curve for your industry.

Increment upgrades are easier to adjust to versus making a

dramatic leap all at once. It doesn't apply just to the adjustments to new technology for your team; it also applies to the costs as well. From a budgetary perspective, it is much easier to budget for small incremental technology upgrades versus paying for a major upgrade in one year. That can significantly impact your profit margin for that year, especially if it has not been one of your company's high performing years to start with.

Even bigger businesses have failed because they got behind in the technology for their industry and just couldn't swallow the capital costs for a major upgrade. As you formulate your strategic plan, you need to make room for technology. After all, its advances are also going to affect how well you can serve the needs of your customers. If you are focused on growth, then you are constantly focusing on the best practices of your industry, and making improvements.

This is why you need to make friends with technology, doing your research, and knowing what is happening, not just in your industry locally, but around the world. It is critical, as a business owner, that you are attending industry conferences and trade shows. Doing so will help you to stay up to date with the technological advances happening, not just in your own neck of the woods but throughout your industry on a global scale.

Doing so will keep you up to date and make sure that you aren't falling behind. After all, incremental changes are great, but only if you know what is out there and can make smart choices based on the direction of the industry as a whole.

Your customers are also going to see what your competitors are doing, and they will expect that same level of convenience or security. Are you able to provide that, or has your inability to embrace technology meant that your customers see you as the dinosaur?

Incubators are available to businesses and are often funded through government programs or grants. These incubators help businesses to do their research, or partner with businesses to provide funding, feedback, or labs to do research work. It can be a great tool to take an idea from your drawing board to the commercial stage, especially for smaller to medium-sized businesses that might not have all the resources available to take on such a big project.

There is so much support out there for businesses, and you need to be active in taking advantage of these tools!

Automation

When it comes to manufacturing, automation has been the name of the game for years. In order to become more efficient, manufacturing has continued to look for methods to improve processes, eliminate inefficiencies, and produce a better product in less time. Look at the automobile industry. From the beginning, when Ford came up with assembly lines, manufacturing has continued to move forward, using technology to give workers the ability to do more, with less personnel.

Many businesses have manual processes that aren't taking advantage of the automation available. When you don't use automation for repetitive tasks, you increase the risk of error, and also increase your costs. I am sure that you can think of various tasks throughout your organization that cost significantly less because you have automated them. As part of your innovation process, be open to the automation of other tasks and processes. Doing so will allow you to reduce labor costs, while maintaining a high level of efficiency and a lower number of errors.

You can also significantly increase your productivity and capacity as well. The initial costs may be higher, but you can save over time, and create more sales because your capacity is greater. Automation should always be part of the budget. It is important to use technology to move your business forward.

Project Management

Have you struggled to implement technology into your business? You know it is a good move and can help your business to move forward, but the process has been painful for your team, and the technology hasn't met your expectations. The reality is that project management is key to the successful implementation of any new technology into your processes or systems.

Project management methodology helps you to implement and innovate much more efficiently. If you can't implement technology, then you can't benefit from it. So many businesses and organizations that I have worked with point to a lack of capital or resources necessary to fully implement new technology, or argue that the process is too overwhelming. This is because they are trying to do too many things without any structure in place. If you use project management methodology, then you are likely to have a better outcome.

I encourage businesses to have their staff trained on two things: project management and quality management. Doing so can improve any implementation of new technology or applications. Otherwise, you will be wasting a whole lot of resources, money, and time that could be spent elsewhere.

CRM & ERP System

The reference here is having an automated system that helps to manage your customer relationship from end to end. It is not just about sales or customers' information in the background. The point of CRM is to take your customer's experience to the next level.

Think of it as a relationship management tool for your entire organization, helping them to access information and critical data throughout the customer's cycle with your business. This is a key piece of technology, which can be a critical part of building a customer experience that compliments your brand. How many times have you called into a company and they weren't able to access information about your order, product, or account history? It was frustrating, was it not?

As a business leader, you need to recognize that your company cannot grow if you do not provide the tools for your team to effectively manage the customer experience. An effective CRM system, tailored to your company, can give you the edge to create a better customer experience with every interaction.

According to Investopedia, enterprise resource planning (ERP) is a process used mostly by manufacturers to manage and integrate important areas of the business, like planning, purchasing, inventory, sales, marketing, finance, and human resources. There are various ERP software available to integrate these functions. ERP implementation is a complex and expensive process; usually, the business has to attain a certain level of complexity and growth before implementing an ERP system.

These systems are also driving changes in technology. One of the businesses I worked with hadn't updated their CRM system in 10 years. They found that the company no longer even supported their system. During those 10 years, they hadn't taken advantage of the incremental changes, new modules, and patches from the provider. As a result, they incurred a cost in the millions to put in a new CRM system.

This dramatic change and large outlay of capital could have been avoided with incremental advances. Keeping up with the technology means allowing small changes to build overtime, instead of shocking your organization with a massive change because your system has become obsolete.

Software Integration

In line with the idea of incremental changes, it is important to keep in mind that your different systems need to be able to interact with each other. A great software package might be able to increase efficiency, but if it doesn't integrate with any of your other systems, then the benefits could be lost, as team members need to input information from one system to another.

Companies fall into this trap where they integrate their software when they bring in new products or technologies; and suddenly, it seems as if they are in a web of software and applications. Training becomes a nightmare, as new and even older employees need to be familiar with multiple programs across various systems, none of which are talking to each other.

Processing times are also increased, because the same information may need to be inputted into multiple systems to get different results, based on the software and applications involved. As a business owner, you can see your bottom line being negatively impacted.

An example of this is one of the big US-based multinational banks. Prior to the financial meltdown, they were one of the biggest banking firms in the world. They grew primarily through acquisitions, which meant, over time, there were layers and layers of software and applications from those businesses. What they did not do very well, over the years, was software integration. Overtime, they had multiple systems, such as legacy systems, new systems, old processing software, and more.

Now they had a problem, because all these products were similar across the globe, but the programs and applications to implement them were totally different. It wasn't efficient, and it wasn't cost effective, plus it hurt them during the financial meltdown. Their new strategy was to cut down on products and create new platforms, which cost millions of dollars. At a time when their business had already taken a hit, their capital expenditures were another impact to the bottom line. Instead of regrouping and setting themselves onto a growth trajectory, they had to spend time correcting this software issue. They weren't the only one, but you can clearly see how this impacted their organization.

Do you want to find yourself in the same position? Then be proactive about integrating new applications and software as you grow your business. Doing so will protect your bottom line, and will positively impact your ability to train your team and serve your customers.

Additionally, if you aren't managing software integration effectively, recognize that your competition is. That entrepreneur is using technology to do it faster and cheaper than you are. Your customers will only be loyal for so long, before jumping ship to the competition. If you can't get it done faster, then you are going to lose. Don't make that mistake; keep software integration a priority as you take advantage of all that technology and innovation have to offer!

CHAPTER 11
Financial Health

There are a few different ways to assess the financial health of your business. When it comes to finance, it is more data-driven than other aspects of your organization. Traditionally, businesses look at the financial performance through the lens of actual financial data, and compare it to the forecasted numbers. You need to be able to set goals and then determine where to get the best bang for your buck by applying the realities of a budget, and allocating accordingly.

Most businesses require regular in-depth reviews of their finances. They could be preparing for a large capital investment, expenses might have significantly increased, or cash reserves might be lower than anticipated. I advise businesses to take a deep dive look at their financial structure every month. You need to do a feedback session and a deep dive to compare to your monthly and quarterly projections.

Additionally, you can do comparisons against historical data for the same time YOY (year over year), to see if you are doing better or worse. There might be reasons to account for the differences, including capital expenditures, revenue numbers, operational costs, etc., but if you don't have those reasons to account for the differences, it can signal that you need to make changes or adjustments in your financial approach to the business, including how you are spending your resources. You need to be willing and able to act, as you become aware of indications that are negatively impacting your business's financial health.

Your financials can also point towards larger trends within your industry, which can indicate that your industry might be suffering a downturn or other trends. When you learn of these trends, you can adjust your business and your product offerings to weather the market's changes effectively. To do this, you need to be able to tap into industry data and trends as benchmarks to compare your business's performance to the immediate competition and industry as a whole. Remember that your financial health can be impacted by the health of your industry, and it is important to be aware of what is going on to avoid making decisions that can negatively impact your business and its ability to grow.

Investors and bankers are going to want to know what your finances look like before they consider loaning you capital, or investing in your business. Therefore, you need to manage your balance sheet closely, because it will indicate your assets and liabilities, as well as the revenue fluctuations over time. When your business has little in the way of assets, and has multiple liabilities, or the revenue and receivables month over month reflect a declining trend, it can negatively impact your access to capital for major improvements, or to meet long-term strategic growth goals. Another critical factor that reflects on financial health is the operating expenses. Most organizations fail to keep these in check, and they can blow up pretty quickly and diminish the margins.

Therefore, it is important to stay on top of trends and the impact of the small changes you are making on a daily and monthly basis. Some of those may be improving your business, while others may not. If you can't measure a change, then don't do it. You need to be able to measure the impact of an initiative to see if it is working or not. If you have multiple initiatives going, you need to be able to measure them individually to determine which are having a positive impact and which ones might be just a drain to your resources.

One way to do this is a champion challenger. Take a small sample of your business process, and implement the change, while the rest of the process maintains the same methods used previously. Essentially, they become the baseline that you can then measure your change against. Now, you can determine what the change is going to do, and based on the results over time, you will get the insights you need, and a true picture of how it is trending. I want you to understand that your challenger group needs to be a decent sample size, and you need to give it time to collect enough data to make reasonable analysis. Depending on the change, a few weeks might be sufficient, but other changes could require months of data to effectively measure the results.

There are a few financial ratios that can provide indication of financial health of a business, which I believe every business needs to look at very closely on a monthly and quarterly basis. There are other ratios that you can look into if you want to do a deeper dive and do some more digging. Below, I am going to talk about these four main financial ratios.

Liquidity ratios—According to Investopedia, *"Liquidity ratios measure a company's ability to pay debt obligations, and its margin of safety, through the calculation of metrics, including the current ratio, quick ratio, and operating cash flow ratio. Current liabilities are analyzed in relation to liquid assets to evaluate the coverage of short-term debts in an emergency. Bankruptcy analysts and mortgage originators use liquidity ratios to evaluate going concern issues, as liquidity* *measurement ratios indicate cash flow positioning."* How liquid is your business? How much cash and easily convertible assets do you have? These ratios help you to determine how much cash you have available to meet short-term expenses and financial needs. Essentially, you need to know that you have enough cash on hand to cover your expenses, and the available funds to tap in case of an emergency or unexpected event. If payments are delayed, it gives you an idea of how long you can cover the business expenses based on the cash and credit available to your organization. As part of your analysis of cash on hand, you need to have a clear credit policy, so your business doesn't become overextended due to payment delays. There must be a balance for the financial success of your business.

Efficiency ratios—This ratio is typically measured over a five-year period. It can give further insight into the business, including collections, cash flow, and inventory turnover. For companies that must carry a lot of inventory, the turnover rate is a critical part of its overall financial efficiency. The longer a product sits on the shelf, the more it is costing your business. In the car industry, for example, the point is to get rid of inventory to make room for newer models and styles. The longer cars sit on their lot, the less newer models they can carry. Is your business inventory-driven? Then it is critical that you use the efficiency ratio to determine how well you are moving inventory, because it could indicate that you need to consider shifting products, or reducing the amount you purchase of slow-selling products, to free up space for quick sellers. This ratio can also assist you in recognizing potential areas of inventory management or changes to your buying strategies. One company I worked with did their inventory management by hand, requiring extra staff to manage fulfillment and inventory tracking. Once they put in a program that allowed for automation, they were able to significantly reduce costs, while increasing the speed of their fulfillment process. Thus, you can eliminate waste and create cost savings for your business.

Profitability ratios—These ratios not only help you to access your financial health but also assist in assessing how your business is doing against other similar businesses— basically, your competition. According to Investopedia, *"Profitability ratios are a class of financial metrics that are used to assess a business's ability to generate earnings compared to its expenses and other relevant costs incurred during a specific period of time."* You can compare ratios over several years because it gives you a better comparison. For example, net profit margin measures how much a company earns after tax, in comparison to its sales. If your competition has a higher profit margin, then it is likely that they are more efficient in delivering their goods and services. These comparisons can help you to see areas where your business could adopt best practices to become more competitive within your industry. Operating profit margin, on the other hand, is determined using taxes and interest paid. This ratio can make your financial picture look quite different, once you factor in those costs of doing business. By analyzing this margin, you can determine the ability of your business to expand in terms of taking on additional debt. When it comes to growth, as an owner, you need to understand how the debt you take on will impact your bottom line and its financial health. Other ratios—ROA (return on assets), ROE (return on equity), and Profit Margins— that fall under this group, can show the return for your shareholders, as well as how your business is weathering various twists and turns within the market.

Leverage ratio—These ratios focus on the long-term solvency of the business, including how much debt you are using to support your business, and your debt to equity ratio. Another example is the debt to asset ratio, which helps to determine how the assets of a business are financed, whether from creditors or your personal investment. In most cases, banks will see a low ratio as good in terms of your business taking on additional debt to pay for growth initiatives or technology upgrades.

There are a variety of online tools to use for calculating these ratios, along with financial advisors and your accounting service. Even members of your finance department could put these ratios together, depending on the size of your business. Every country has different avenues for sharing industry data, so determine the best places to find your industry's data to analyze your business in terms of the industry's statistics. Some industries also have their own associations that can be tapped for data without breaking the bank.

Using these ratios, you can better understand not only your own business and benchmark against competition and industry standards, but the macro or micro environment that you are operating in. Keeping a log of the changes is critical to understanding the impact on your ratios.

Numbers are important to understanding your financial health, but they only tell half the story. The rest of the story is beyond the numbers. As a business, you need to look at other variables as well, beyond these data points. It is one thing to crunch the data, but it is another to understand what caused that data and the factors influencing those numbers. For instance, if you changed locations, the impact of that move is going to be reflected in your numbers. It could mean that you saw a dip in sales during the move, but they rebounded as the year continued. The point is that the dip would be a potential cause for alarm if you didn't know about the factors that may have contributed to that dip. Other dynamics could have positively impacted your business, causing a spike in sales.

Politics can also impact your business because of their role in terms of labor. For instance, governments can impact the minimum wage, which can increase your labor costs. Businesses, particularly small ones, may find themselves unable to remain competitive in terms of pricing, thus putting some of those companies out of business. Legislation can have long-term impacts that might not be immediately apparent but can negatively impact your business operating costs.

As a business owner, the point is to recognize that there is more to analyzing your business than just running these ratios. You have to take all of these factors into account when making strategic decisions for the growth of your business, but at the same time, recognize that these ratios can give you indications about the health of your business in wake of different internal and external factors.

Capital Allocation and Budgeting

For a business to be financially viable, you need to recognize that you aren't going to be able to fund everything that you want to do. Your business is going to have multiple needs, and all of them are going to require capital resources. Obviously, your resources are only going to cover so much. As part of your growth strategy, you need to focus your resources where you can get the most accomplished. I encourage you to revisit your strategic plan and your goals for your business, both in the short term and long term.

As you create your budget, you need to consider those goals. You might spend a large chunk of resources to accomplish a short-term goal, but what impact will that have on your long-term goals? Capital allocation is about creating priorities and recognizing that some priorities will not give you the most bang for your buck. ROI analysis can be key to making decisions regarding the initiatives that you choose to take on.

When you create your budget and allocate resources, you want to maximize every dollar. Financial waste can kill a business, limiting its ability to take advantage of growth opportunities because of a lack of resources. Don't do this to your business, but be strategic in determining how to spend your capital to make quality choices for your business.

Finance is always going to be the voice of reason in your business. You might want to take on everything and pursue every new technology that becomes available, but finance makes you zero in on what will work best for your business from a numbers perspective, and help you to make informed decisions to potentially maximize the return on your capital investments.

Creating a budget, prior to the start of your next fiscal year, helps you to plan for what is coming down the pipeline in terms of potential capital expenditures to replace equipment or for staff training, as well as initiatives that you want to pursue throughout the year. Departments also need to be given their budgets, as well as the expectations you have for the year, in terms of productivity and goals to accomplish.

Budgeting involves your strategic plan; you need to determine your priorities before you can allocate resources. So many businesses don't take their long-term goals into account when determining their budget, and they underfund areas of their business necessary to reach those long-term goals. The budget for your company cannot be created in a vacuum; it requires input from your key managers and department heads. Doing so will help you to understand their needs, and weigh those financial needs against the other needs within the company.

Another important point is that when you define the initiatives for the year, and the budget for those initiatives, you need to stick to that budget. Your financial health will be compromised if you routinely go over budget, putting your business deeper into debt, without a justifiable ROI.

Throughout this book, I have continued to come back to the importance of planning, and your budget is just one more area where this is the case. Yes, it is important to have resources for emergencies, but you should be able to consistently meet your budget, or even be slightly under-budget, by creating operational efficiencies.

Your strategic plan and initiatives will also guide your growth in terms of whether you seek additional capital, either from investors or the bank, or even from using your personal resources. That planning needs to be done and then evaluated every month or every quarter, to make sure that departments are on track regarding your budget and the initiatives they have been assigned. You do not want to get to the end of the year and find that you are significantly over budget because you didn't recognize that the costs of pursuing an initiative were more than you originally budgeted. Instead, by evaluating your financial position throughout the year, you can make the necessary adjustments to keep your budget and initiatives on track.

Another point to make here is that you need to evaluate whether an initiative is having the effect you wanted. If it isn't, you could choose to not move forward on that project, thus cutting your losses to what you have already spent, instead of continuing to spend money on something that is not going to have the impact you anticipated on your business. The resources already spent on the failing initiative are part of the sunk cost, and you have to stop putting any additional resources into it.

Fixed Costs and Operating Expenses

Fixed costs and operating expenses are the costs of doing business. They can include overhead for your space and machinery. While some of these costs will be part of your monthly expenses continually, others might not be, or can be negotiated to reduce the overhead costs of your business.

Operating expenses and variable costs are ones that you can manage more effectively because you can negotiate or even cut down the spending in those areas. One example of this could be travel costs. You can put processes in place to keep travel costs down in terms of when you book, and the airlines or hotels used. Other costs can also be adjusted, especially those that are contracted. When you negotiate the contract, look to keep your costs down wherever possible.

Day-to-day operations, including office supplies, can be another area where you can reduce expenses. Running lean can positively impact the bottom line. When you plan and prepare to run lean, you need to look for process and procedure improvements, including automation, to increase the efficiency while managing your costs. Small improvements can result in big dollar savings over the year.

Forecasting

Forecasting for the next year can be done late in the 3rd quarter; by the end of the year, you have the numbers finalized and can begin planning for next year. Once that forecast is done, it is locked, and you build your assumptions around that forecast. It can be a tool to compare your progress throughout the year with where you forecasted to be. The point of these tools is to keep you from running your business from a firefighter mentality, where you cannot grow because you are constantly putting out fires. When you are in that situation, it can also mean you are spending more than you need to, and you aren't sticking to any budget. The financial health of your business can be negatively impacted as a result.

Taxation

Taxes can be a big expense for a business. As a business owner, it is critical to get good advice regarding your tax situation, and to make sure that you are paying all the necessary taxes but also assessing your tax situation for any tax breaks or credits that are applicable to your business.

There may be programs for tax breaks based on innovations or new technology that you may have implemented. Do your homework to determine what qualifies for your business. Essentially, you need to look for legal ways to lower your taxes, from exemptions to credits, or tax breaks, based on your location.

Cities, counties, states/provinces, and feds all have different tax breaks and incentives meant to encourage businesses to grow in those areas and contribute to the local economy. Don't be quick to assume that none of those incentives apply to your business. Working with your accountant, you can identify the potential breaks your company qualifies for, and then submit the necessary proof or paperwork.

Green or environmentally friendly programs can also offer tax incentives, but I find that many businesses are not aware of these programs. Again, I cannot stress enough the importance of finding out what is available, and determining if your business qualifies. You might be surprised at the tax break options out there.

Realignment Based on Strategy and Lifecycle

Every year, when you look at your business, you need to look at how it performed— whether it was good, bad, or ugly. In the process, you can find areas where you can realign your business to address your strategic plan and goals. There might be areas where your business appeared to drift off course, and realignments can help you to make those necessary course corrections.

This realignment could even include reorganizing departments, finding teams that have synergy, and combining resources to achieve the objectives and goals of your strategic plan. Every year, I find businesses that don't make these realignments on a yearly basis, which could be detrimental to the business. Yearly changes can be more incremental, whereas when you wait, it is a much bigger shock to the departments and teams within your business. Inevitably, when you wait, it ends up costing your business more, and it is more disruptive to your employees and your corporate culture.

Another important point is that realignment could mean redefining roles within your company. You might be able to automate some tasks or make changes to processes that allow the work of several people to be done by just a couple, or even one. While it might mean laying off employees, there is a cost savings by being able to do more with less, and that includes less employees. However, to save on overhead, no changes in staff should be done at the expense of the customer experience, because doing so is likely to drive away customers.

The reality is that you should be looking at realigning all aspects of your business throughout the year, particularly when it comes to processes. Don't wait until a specific quarter to adjust, because it can end up costing your business more in the long run. I cannot stress enough the importance of regularly gauging the health of your business and creating a culture of constant improvement. Doing so will have a positive impact on your ability to reach your strategic goals and create constant growth.

The lifecycle of your business is critically tied to the growth of your business. When you start out, you might not have much in the way of resources, employees, or even customers. As your business grows, those needs change, and you find yourself with more capital available, a need for a larger staff, and a significantly larger customer base.

As a result, realignment needs to be a constant process to ensure that you are meeting the needs of your business, now and into the future. Granted, you might find multiple areas where you need to adjust, but this is where your strategic plan comes in. Using that to help you prioritize the changes, you can shift your business on an incremental basis, and after a few years, look back to see a significant change. You need to provide your business with the thought leadership with futuristic viewpoint.

Throughout the last few chapters, I have focused on how you can gauge the health of your business, and the importance of creating an environment of constant change to keep your growth constant. Finally, I want to talk about government programs, particularly how you can build a relationship with your local and federal government stakeholders to create or maintain growth.

CHAPTER 12

Doing Business with the Government

One of the first and most important things to remember about doing business with the government is that there is going to be more of everything: more hoops to jump through, more red tape, and definitely more paperwork. However, doing business with the government can have its benefits in terms of grants or funding that assists your R&D, if your business is part of a priority sector.

Depending on how you want your business to grow, the government can be a viable opportunity. Throughout the following pages, I am going to talk about some key areas where you can work with the government, including potential benefits, but also things you need to keep in mind.

To be honest, when I talk to businesses about doing business with the government, there is a focus primarily on selling to the government, and its procurement process. There is often little thought about the other opportunities available working with the government. I am going to discuss a few of them below. Keep in mind that working with a consultant can help you to successfully navigate the rules and regulations in your local area, state, or country.

Granted, it can seem that the bureaucracy of working with the government can make it more of a hassle than an opportunity, but the options below are not necessarily so labor intensive as to put them out of your reach. In fact, some government programs can help your business to reach its strategic goals, promoting growth and moving your business forward.

Government Funding and Grants

These are huge for businesses because business owners don't often realize how much support the government offers, particularly for small to medium-sized businesses. Funding and grants, some of which do not have to be returned or paid back, are available to help grow the business, or there is funding available where you pay the debt back over a longer period of time, with limited to no interest.

A lot of times, businesses do not invest in finding out about these opportunities. I am surprised at how many businesses are not aware of these funding opportunities; in many cases, they are simply too wrapped up in the day-to-day firefighting within their own business, and the focus isn't there. I advise business owners constantly to take the time to invest in these programs. Simply put, it is worth the effort because of the opportunities it can afford your business.

The government uses agents in various industries to help connect businesses with its programs, so if you are looking to take your business to the next stage, it is worth seeking out one of these individuals to help you in accessing the options available.

Additionally, there are private consulting firms that specialize in government funding and grant programs. They can provide the assistance you need to connect with the right program for your business, while allowing you to continue to focus your attention on running your business. They understand the process of application, what businesses are going to qualify, and the information you will need to provide. These firms also are up to date on the mandates from the government, and areas they want to focus on, so they can help those businesses connect with the government. Tapping these firms for their expertise can be a great way to explore these potential opportunities.

If you have the resources internally, you can begin the process of doing the research and creating the relationships to move forward with these programs. However, most small businesses do not have those types of resources available, so taking advantage of private firms that already have these relationships is a viable route to consider. They can help you through the application process from end to end, so you can remain in compliance in terms of your reporting requirements.

While the reporting requirements may seem frustrating and arduous, keep in mind that the government is accountable to taxpayers, and needs to be sure that the money and resources are being used appropriately. Therefore, while it can be time-consuming, the availability of these programs allows businesses to grow that might otherwise struggle to find capital or resources in the private marketplace.

Additionally, there is a lot of support for innovation. Therefore, if you are looking to do R&D, be willing to look into government options, as well as third-parties. They can help you to fund your research, giving your business the boost to move forward with a new product, services, or application. The point is that these grants and funding options are there to provide support to small and medium-sized businesses—those that are the backbone to the economy.

Government Backed Organizations and Programs

These are the ones funded by the government but are not government agencies. Instead, they are non-profit third parties that work closely with the government to achieve various objectives within various sectors and industries. As a result, they are available to provide options for R&D, testing, and incubator space to assist businesses in moving forward with their innovation efforts.

Their offerings are often available at no-to-low-cost for small to medium-sized businesses, if those businesses fall in the category or sector they are trying to promote. Cost-sharing is also another option when working with these organizations, depending on the project and the size of the project, as well as the anticipated outcome.

One thing that I highly encourage businesses to do, even if working with these government-backed agencies, is to have a contract and non-disclosure agreement in place. These documents will protect your proprietary information, as well as the development work, and will make sure that you own the IP (Intellectual Property) rights for the products and services being developed for your business. There could be a dispute at the end of the program about who owns what, because these contracts and documents were not in place before the work began. I encourage you to have this conversation up front and get everything down on paper before the work begins. In many cases, you might have to negotiate to own the IP rights.

Another way these third-parties can assist is by helping you to find the right funding or industry expertise, such as manufacturing options. These third parties work closely with industry experts, so if you are looking to expand outside of the current realm of your business, they can help you find the right experts to move forward with that expansion, at no-to-minimal cost.

Networking is part of growth, and these third parties can often help two businesses that might have synergy to connect with each other. They might also connect a business that has a need with another business that can fill the need. Again, the point is that these third parties provide those networking opportunities, which can provide another platform of growth and a mutually beneficial relationship.

Chambers of Commerce and Boards of Trade

These are organizations that work very closely with businesses, as well as the government and various ministries of the government. They are frequently involved in trade missions, both to other countries and for dignitaries visiting from other countries as well. These groups are also lobbying the government, providing a voice for various industries. They are really good at giving feedback to the government and being a sounding board on various policies.

Lots of SMEs are not taking advantage of this avenue, both in terms of lobbying and recognizing what is coming down the pipeline. These groups are keyed in, not just at the state and federal levels but even down at the local government level. Thus, they provide access for businesses to contribute and have a voice in new laws, regulations, and community development master plans.

I encourage you to become an active member of your local chamber of commerce, as well as any trade boards or organizations. This membership will give you a voice in your community and the developments that can impact your business and its growth. There is a lot of synergy that can come from these networking and feedback opportunities. The more active you are, the more clued in you will be about what is going on in your community and government, as well as how it can or will impact your business.

Colleges and Universities

I hear constantly from businesses how hard it is to find good talent. Depending on the industry or area that you are in, this problem could be better or worse. Still, one of the best ways to tap into talent is by connecting with your local colleges and universities. Instead of waiting for them to graduate and come to you, your business is on their radar because they are building a relationship with you while still in school.

You can provide internship programs, mentoring, and case studies to help these students learn more about your business, and build ties that will bring them to your company right out of school. Let's face it, these programs are churning out graduates, annually, semi-annually, and in some cases, even quarterly. It is a resource that can provide your team with fresh blood, new skill-sets, and the talent to innovate and move your business to the next level.

Another option is to have a group of students come to your business and complete a project as part of their class work. You would otherwise have to pay for the project to be completed by a consultant, or at the expense of using your own team. By pairing with the college, you get their students' assistance, with limited costs, and the students receive valuable experience and an entry on their resume—and both sides win. Iain McNab, Dean of the Faculty of Applied Science and Technology at Sheridan College, always provides this one caveat: if you are under a delivery deadline to a client, or if it is a mission critical project, then don't use a team from the college or university. They will not be able to guarantee timely delivery of the project or the desired outcome, as it's a student led project. However, if you don't have strict timelines, or it is a smaller research project, you can take advantage of building a relationship with the college.

In many cases, all it takes is a call to a department head at the college to start the ball rolling. Using this option can help you to move products and services forward, while maximizing your resources in the process.

Tax Breaks and Subsidies

Again, these go hand in hand with the other programs and offerings available from the government. Using these tax breaks and subsidies, the government can support key sectors or use them to support small and medium businesses. In some cases, the local chambers of commerce or trade boards have lobbied to receive support from the government. I cannot iterate enough the importance of connecting with these groups, as you can then be aware of what funding has been lobbied for, and take advantage of those subsidies and tax breaks.

Some of your tax breaks can even be related to research and development, particularly for sectors that the government wants to see expand even further. It could essentially give you a take break for your R&D budget. Ask your accountant to do the research to find out what tax breaks you might qualify for.

Many small businesses don't get all the tax breaks they are eligible for because they don't know about them, their accountant doesn't know, and no one thinks to ask. In a small business, that is leaving funding and capital for potential growth in the hands of the government. Be willing to take the time to do your homework to benefit from the tax breaks and subsidies that you are eligible for.

Priority Sectors

Businesses need to look at what the priority sectors are for the government and if there is any synergy between their business and these priorities. It also could be a case of doing similar work, but your business doesn't quite fall into one of these sectors. Could you refocus your business to take advantage of the opportunities available as part of these priority sectors?

It could be done through expansion of your business to take advantage of these funding opportunities, allowing you to find your next niche or level of growth. Once you do so, then you can tap into the support available through the government for these sectors or industries.

Selling to the Government

This section is the one that most businesses are interested in and what frequently comes to mind when it comes to doing business with the government. Now, there are four areas where you can sell to the government as a business: the federal, state, regional, and municipal city levels.

The point that I stress to businesses is that you must know the process. For many businesses looking to provide a product or service to the government, they are not aware of who they should contact, how they make them aware of their offerings, and how the procurement process works once the government decides to do business with you.

It is important to know what the buying process includes. Most governments provide direction on their website, so it is important to do your homework and research before you start contacting the government and attempting to get your first meeting. Most of the time, it is a lack of understanding of the process, or thinking the process is too complicated, that keeps businesses from making a connection that can result in increased sales for their business.

The government, particularly in Canada, is one of the biggest consumers of the goods and services of small businesses. In fact, the Canadian government has purchased roughly 43% of its goods and services from small businesses, to the tune of $20 billion. Those are huge numbers when it comes to purchasing. It makes sense to do business with the government if you have the right products and services to offer. You just need to understand what the process looks like and who you need to connect with, along with what they are focused on buying now, and who they want to buy from.

Therefore, it is important to get your business into the databases of these ministries and agencies because, if you aren't in the database, then they are not likely to even look at your business from a purchasing standpoint. Sometimes the way that you create history with the purchasing department is to become a subcontractor to the prime contractor, building a relationship that will allow you to eventually become the main contractor.

Part of creating that relationship is through networking and promoting your business. Get to those meetings, make the connections, and learn the process. Doing so will give your company the leg up it needs to move forward in making the government a customer of your organization.

There are also third-party consulting firms that specialize in this field, helping you to work through the process effectively, including keeping you aware of key dates in the procurement process. Finally, you need to recognize that your proposal is going to be part of a bidding process. Therefore, you need to make sure that your proposal is competitive and meets all the necessary requirements. You need to understand what they are going to require, and that you can meet the demands of the contract you are trying to receive. Take the time to go to seminars and workshops from the government, which help businesses to understand the process.

There is a whole lot of support available from the government to encourage businesses to export. Those resources can help you get access to additional markets outside of your home country, and provide guidance regarding the culture and trade agreements. They can also help you with the exporting process. As I mentioned previously, if you don't understand the process, you can make mistakes that cost you time and money.

Being active with the government can also help you to go on trade missions, where you can interact with other businesses outside of your country, and create those connections to expand your markets. It is a really good avenue to network and build those partnerships.

Additionally, if you aren't successful the first time, don't be willing to write off the government as a growth opportunity. With the right effort, you can tap resources, customers, and the markets available. If you are willing to do the legwork at the beginning, working with the government can be a fantastic option for growth and reaching your strategic goals.

Working with the right consultant, you can tap into all these areas, using their connections and experience to provide a growth platform for your business. If you are interested in working with me, I invite you to contact me at my website (insert website). I would love to be able to help you find the right avenues to grow your business and push you to the next level.

CHAPTER 13

Grow Your Business, Thinking Big

No matter the size of your business, growth is necessary to keep your business successful. Those businesses that don't focus on creating and sustaining growth eventually find themselves falling behind the industry and closing their doors.

The point of this book is to help small to medium business owners to focus on the areas in which they need to concentrate, in order to facilitate growth. Those big corporate businesses are constantly working on these areas, and they are driving the industry. Don't let the size of large corporate companies scare you into limiting the potential of your own company.

Your strategic plan needs to be the first thing you focus on. As a business owner, you can't know what you need unless you know where you are headed. Throughout these chapters, I have continued to focus on how critical it is to set goals and be willing to adjust to the changing needs of your organization, your team, your customers, and your marketplace.

Those businesses that are unwilling to make changes and adjustments might not feel the consequences right away, but they will eventually, and it could spell disaster for their business.

As the leader of your company, you need to understand that if you aren't focused on continually growing your business, then you are sentencing it to a slow and painful death. Businesses need to grow to continue to be successful. If you make the same amount of sales, year over year, then the cost of doing business will eventually outstrip the amount of money your business is bringing in. It is the reality of an economic climate that includes inflation and an ever-improving standard of living.

I wanted this to be a reference, a way for you to continually find areas to improve. By focusing on continual and never-ending improvement, you are encouraging your team to always look for innovative ways to do business. No business should be satisfied with doing what they have always done. I have tried to give you the tools necessary to examine your own business and determine if you have fallen into this trap.

Along the way, I want you to recognize that no business is perfect. Even those businesses that are successful and growing must continue to innovate and look for improvements in their processes. They must respond to changing conditions in the marketplace and economy. They are also dealing with global competitors. Yet these companies continue to grow because of their willingness to continue moving forward.

I encourage you to look for avenues to tap expertise beyond your organization. Best practices discussed at trade shows, industry seminars, and training webinars are just a few ways to tap into the expertise of others. Also, be willing to look for a consultant who can provide you the benefit of their experience and knowledge, both within your industry and from outside of it.

Innovation doesn't have to be limited to how things are done in your organization or industry. Looking outside of your industry can be the catalyst to creating a new product or process, one that might not have occurred to anyone else. Connections are not always obvious, but if you are willing to try new things and ideas, it can really pay off for your company.

I wish you continued growth and success in your business! May you be able to take your organization to the next point on your strategic plan, and beyond!

ABOUT THE AUTHOR

Rony is a global citizen, having lived and worked in three continents. He earned his Bachelors in Economics in India and MBA in International Business in New Zealand where he was the Valedictorian of his graduating class.

Throughout his career, Rony has gained extensive expertise in leadership, operations management, process improvement and automation. He loves helping his private business clients to grow their business through operational efficiencies & transformational leadership. He was inspired to write this book while consulting as the Senior Business Advisor with the Ministry of Economic Development & Growth, at Ontario Provincial Services in Canada.

Prior to starting his journey around the globe, Rony was an officer in the Indian Army and a qualified instructor in Counter Terrorism & Jungle Warfare. He is the recipient of the prestigious Army Medal for leadership & valour from the honourable President of India.

Rony is an active person who loves the outdoors, sports, and was a semi-professional dancer who won international level dance competitions. He is an avid traveller and loves to explore different cultures and the planet's diversity.